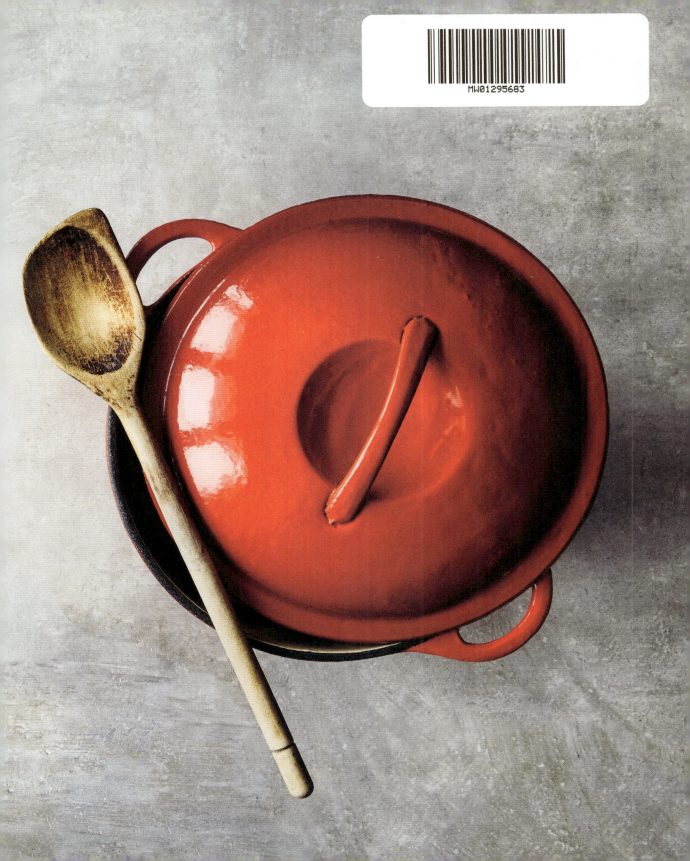

the Dutch Oven
COOKBOOK

the Dutch Oven COOKBOOK

60 recipes for one-pot cooking

LOUISE PICKFORD

Photography by
IAN WALLACE

RYLAND PETERS & SMALL
LONDON • NEW YORK

Senior Designer Toni Kay
Senior Editor Gillian Haslam
Editorial Director Julia Charles
Head of Production Patricia Harrington
Production Manager Gordana Simakovic
Art Director Leslie Harrington
Publisher Cindy Richards

Food and Prop Stylist Louise Pickford
Indexer Hilary Bird

First published in 2021 by
Ryland Peters & Small
20–21 Jockey's Fields
London WC1R 4BW
and
341 E 116th St
New York NY 10029
www.rylandpeters.com

10 9 8 7 6 5 4 3 2 1

Text copyright © Louise Pickford 2021
Design and photographs copyright
© Ryland Peters & Small 2021

ISBN: 978-1-78879-389-6

The author's moral rights have been asserted. All rights reserved. No part of this publication may be reproduced, stored in a retrieval system, or transmitted in any form or by any means, electronic, mechanical, photocopying, or otherwise, without the prior permission of the publisher.

A CIP record for this book is available from the British Library.

US Library of Congress cataloging-in-publication data has been applied for.

Printed and bound in China

NOTES
• Both American (Imperial plus US cups) and British (Metric) measurements and ingredients are included in these recipes for your convenience, however it is important to work with one set of measurements and not alternate between the two within a recipe.
• All spoon measurements are level unless otherwise specified.
• All eggs are large (US) or medium (UK), unless specified as large, in which case US extra-large should be used. Uncooked or partially cooked eggs should not be served to the very old, frail, young children, pregnant women or those with compromised immune systems.
• When a recipe calls for the zest of citrus fruit, buy unwaxed fruit and wash well before using. If you can only find treated fruit, scrub well in warm soapy water before using.
• Ovens should be preheated to the specified temperatures. We recommend using an oven thermometer. If using a fan-assisted oven, adjust temperatures according to the manufacturer's instructions.

Contents

Introduction	6
SOUPS	10
FISH & SEAFOOD	32
MEAT	54
POULTRY	80
VEGETABLE DISHES	102
BAKING & DESSERTS	124
Index	142
Acknowledgments	144

Introduction

I grew up watching my mother cook amazing stews and pot roasts in a cast-iron Dutch oven, or a casserole dish as we called it in the UK. It was so heavy that as a kid I couldn't pick it up empty, let alone when full of deliciousness!

In today's high-convenience, hi-tech world where we demand our designer items perform a dozen different tasks at once, I'll take my 35-year-old hand-me-down Dutch oven over pretty much anything new and sleek. So, what is it about this centuries-old, classic, simple yet beautifully elegant cast-iron pot that makes it many cooks' essential piece of kitchen equipment? It is, of course, its versatility and durability.

The shape of the pot and its weight make it ideal for searing meat over a high heat and then lowering the heat to maintain an evenly distributed, lower temperature, for longer. But this is just the tip of the iceberg. A Dutch oven should not be reserved simply for weekend slow cooking, it can and should be used regularly for every type of cooking, from those stews and pot roasts to bakes, cakes, stir-fries, deep-fried dishes, stovetop braises, and even delicious pies. It is a truly versatile cooking pot and in this book I will share with you 60 of my favorite Dutch oven dishes. I have experimented with different cooking methods and developed recipes from around the world, as far and wide as Asia, Europe, South America, and the US. Its range is broad.

HISTORY

It is perhaps in the US that the Dutch oven has found its place in the hearts and homes of most cooks. Tracing its history is fascinating and in the same way that produce was traded and recipes shared around the world, so were cooking pots.

As its name suggests, it was first made by the Dutch in the 17th century (where it is called a braadpan), yet the early ovens were made of copper and brass rather than iron. It was an English craftsman who took the design back to Britain and began using cast iron to produce a cheaper and more dynamic pot. Early Dutch and British settlers and explorers brought their pots with them to America, arriving on the east coast and gradually traveling west across the vastness of the continent.

With its wide rim and straight sides, often gently sloping at the base, the shape has barely changed over the years (although oval and shallower versions have been added). In the early years, because it was used to cook over an open fire rather than on a stovetop or in an oven, three legs were added, allowing it to sit over rather than on the fire, and we find slightly different versions of this worldwide, including the US, South Africa, Australia, the Far East, and even Russia, where early settlers and nomads prized their cast-iron pans for their durability and versatility. The three-legged versions are still popular today with campers the world over.

Dutch ovens became so prized in the US that their value increased and many would be passed down through families as heirlooms (including Mary Ball Washington, mother of US president George Washington). In old TV westerns you often see a cast-iron pot hanging from cowboy wagons. These campfire pans soon evolved to include a slightly inverted, domed lid so that hot charcoal could be shoveled on top, giving it a more uniform internal heat and a functional oven. This is likely when cooks first started to bake bread in their Dutch ovens.

It wasn't until the early 20th century that the French company Le Creuset developed an enamel coating for their cocotte (the French name) to prevent the cast iron from rusting. New shapes, as well as different colors, began to emerge, with variations in individual sizes plus oval and shallow round pots ideal for sautéing.

It is a testament to the utility of this internationally loved cooking pot that it remains as treasured, well used, and highly valued today as it was centuries ago, when it would often have been the only cooking vessel available in which to cook your every meal.

Discovering I could use my Dutch oven as a wok was especially pleasing, as I hadn't thought of this before. As long as you keep your pan well seasoned (see right) and you get it really hot before adding the ingredients, it stir-fries like a dream.

And those stews... Anyone who has cooked with a Dutch oven for some time will know just how great the flavor of the food will be, and it just seems to get better over the years. It is a very special thing indeed. Is there anything this good old pot can't do? No, I think it's perfect.

INVESTMENT

Purchasing a Dutch oven requires a little thought, but although expensive, given their durability, you will probably only buy one or two in a lifetime, so it is worth getting the right one for your needs.

There are two main types available (with many variations within each type)—cast iron or enamel-coated cast iron, both of which I use in this book.

As a general rule, cast-iron ovens are cheaper than their enameled counterparts. Although they basically do the same thing, the enameled pan (literally a cast-iron pot coated inside and out with enamel) is slightly easier to care for. Both can be used for all types of cooking except broiling/grilling or campfire cooking, which is not recommended for the enamel-coated pan.

The enamel can chip if the edge of the pan is knocked, however it does not need to be seasoned in order to prevent rusting. Enamel-coated pans are non-porous and although less likely to burn, cleaning them is easier and more gentle than for their cast-iron cousins. And if you like a little color in your kitchen, then enameled pans win hands down. They come in the most glorious range of colors, whereas cast-iron black is, well, black.

Both types come in a multitude of sizes, from mini individual ovens to enormous 8-quart/litre options and pretty much everything in between. There are round and oval pans as well as those with shorter sides, ideal for sautés, braises, and pies. There are several well-known manufacturers and the prices vary from one to the other. The larger the pan, the more expensive. My advice is to ask yourself what you will use it for: what type

USES

As well as stews and long, slow roasting, your Dutch oven is ideal for steaming, whether you use a second dish inside the oven or place food directly on a rack above water or a broth. The heavy lid is perfect for keeping the steam inside the pan.

It is good for deep-frying as the pan's very stability (due to its weight) feels so much more secure to the reluctant deep-fryer. Once the required temperature is reached, reducing the heat to low allows you to maintain an even temperature for longer without needing to adjust it up or down.

Stovetop braising is equally as successful as oven braising as the thickness of the pan base allows us to cook long and slow over a low heat without fear of juices burning and sticking to the inside base of the pan.

of cooking do you do? How many people do you regularly cook for? Will you want to use it on a campfire? Is the climate where you live warm and moist or hot and dry? The more informed you are, the better choice you are likely to make.

PREPARATION, CLEANING & STORAGE

If you buy a new Dutch oven, it will come with instructions on how to prepare it before use, how to clean, and how to store, so follow these. However, many of us buy second-hand pans or receive them as hand-me-downs, so here is my best practise for cleaning and storing both types of pan. The better you care for your Dutch oven, the longer it will last and the longer it will continue to produce some of the most delicious dishes you will ever eat.

ENAMEL-COATED CAST-IRON OVEN

Simply using soapy water and a soft sponge to clean your pan will usually suffice, but from time to time we need to get a little more forceful. Make sure your pan is cool. Add a little dishwashing soap, hot water and a couple of tablespoons of baking soda/bicarbonate of soda, then set aside for 15 minutes. Use a plastic scraper to scrape off any stubborn bits. Rinse under cold water and use a soft, wet sponge and a little extra soap to scrub gently at any remaining bits. Rinse again.

For a burnt-on mess or heavy brown staining, make a paste with baking soda/bicarbonate of soda and a little hot water. Spread this over those areas with the sponge. Cover the pan and let sit for several hours, then add a little more hot water and use your soft sponge to rub away the stains. This should leave the pan clean and fresh. Rinse the pan thoroughly under hot water and leave to drain well. Make sure it is completely dry before storing it.

Store your pan partially covered with the lid (you may wish to use a layer of paper towel between the pan and lid) in a cupboard. Always rinse and dry before using it again. There is no need to season an enamel-coated Dutch oven.

CAST-IRON OVEN

Here you can be more robust with your cleaning. After each use, wipe the pan clean with a paper towel and allow it to dry thoroughly. For stains and sticky bits, you can be vigorous. Fill your pan with water and place on the heat, bringing the water to the boil. Remove from the heat and set aside to cool, to loosen the residue. Pour away the water and use a brush or chainmail sponge to rub away stubborn bits of food or stains, adding a little dishwashing soap if needed. When clean, rinse the pan thoroughly with warm water. Dry it well with plenty of paper towels (or place in a warm oven for 10 minutes or so) to make sure it is completely dry.

To season it for storage, pour a teaspoon or two of cooking oil into the pan and wipe all over, inside and out (except for the base), using a paper towel, wiping away any excess. When completely dry, place it in a cupboard with the lid partially covering it, using paper or a clean dish towel between lid and pan. Wipe over the interior of the pan with more paper towel before using it the next time.

RECIPES

All recipes in the book have been tested in the deeper style of ovens rather than the shallow sautéing pans. I used individual pots as well as large round and oval pots and opted for the middle range of sizes in the hope of covering all bases. I do use small 8-oz/250-ml capacity dishes for several recipes (and give advice on using a larger pan if you don't have small ones) and the majority of recipes use a 4–6 quart/litre Dutch oven (both round and oval), as well as a few recipes that use 2–3 quart/litre pans.

Pan sizing differs for each manufacturer. Some give imperial or metric liquid capacity, whereas others give diameter measurements. I have used capacity in all my recipes, as well as a couple of diameters for cakes or baked dishes which require a more specific size. Don't worry if you only have one size of pan—it is fine to adapt the recipes and as a general rule, providing your oven is the same capacity or larger than the one stated in a recipe, you will be fine. Otherwise you can adjust the recipe quantities as required for a smaller pan.

I didn't cook any of my dishes over a campfire but if you plan to do this, please ensure you use a cast-iron pan rather than an enamel-coated pan.

SOUPS

Baked French onion soup with Gruyère topping

Slowly braised onions are truly one of life's pleasures, especially in this classic, comforting soup, with its topping of melted cheese. For vegetarians, if you are happy eating cheese, simply replace the beef or chicken stock with vegetable stock.

5 tablespoons/75 ml extra virgin olive oil

2 lb. 4 oz./1 kg onions, thinly sliced

2 garlic cloves, finely chopped

2 teaspoons freshly chopped thyme

½ cup/125 ml fruity red wine

4 cups/1 litre beef stock or chicken stock (see page 19)

½ French baguette

⅔ cup/75 g grated Gruyère

2 tablespoons grated Parmesan

sea salt and freshly ground black pepper

SERVES 4

Preheat the oven to 400°F/180°C fan/200°C/Gas 6.

Heat the oil in a 4-quart/litre Dutch oven over a medium heat and gently fry the onions, garlic, and thyme with a little salt and pepper for 25 minutes until really soft and lightly golden, stirring frequently to prevent the onions from burning.

Add the wine, bring to the boil, and boil for 5 minutes or until evaporated, then pour in the stock. Bring back to the boil and season to taste.

Cut the bread into slices ½ inch/1 cm thick and arrange over the top of the soup. Scatter over the Gruyère and Parmesan cheeses and transfer the pan to the preheated oven. Bake uncovered for 10–15 minutes until the soup is bubbling and the cheese melted and golden. If you wish, you can brown the top of the cheese under a hot broiler/grill.

Cool for 10 minutes before serving.

White bean & rosemary soup with bacon pangrattato

Pangrattato is an Italian fried breadcrumb garnish, often scattered over a dish of cooked pasta. Here, combined with crispy fried bacon, it provides both crunch and flavor to the finished bean soup. If you prefer to cook your own beans from scratch rather than using canned ones, follow the recipe on page 120 and replace the stock in the recipe below with the cooking liquid from the beans.

4 tablespoons/60 ml olive oil, plus extra to serve

1 large onion, chopped

2 garlic cloves, crushed

2 tablespoons freshly chopped rosemary

12 oz./350 g potatoes, such as Yukon Gold, Russet, Desiree, or King Edward, diced into ½-inch/1-cm cubes

2 x 14-oz./400-g cans cannellini or haricot beans, drained and rinsed (see introduction)

4 cups/1 litre chicken stock (see page 19) or vegetable stock

2 bay leaves

sea salt and freshly ground black pepper

BACON PANGRATTATO

4 tablespoons/60 ml olive oil

4½ oz./125 g slices/rashers of bacon, rind removed and diced

1 large garlic clove, crushed

3½ oz./100 g day-old bread (without crusts)

2 tablespoons freshly chopped flat-leaf parsley

SERVES 4–6

Heat the oil in a 4-quart/litre Dutch oven over a medium heat and fry the onion, garlic, and rosemary for 5 minutes until lightly golden. Add the potatoes and beans, stir well, and then add the stock, bay leaves and a little salt and pepper. Bring to the boil, then lower the heat and simmer gently for 15–20 minutes until the potatoes are tender.

Meanwhile, make the pangrattato. Heat the oil in a medium skillet/frying pan over a high heat. Add the bacon and fry for 2–3 minutes until crisp and golden. Remove the pan from the heat and using a slotted spoon, remove the bacon from the oil, set aside. Add the garlic to the hot oil off the heat and set aside for 10 minutes to flavor it. Remove and discard the garlic.

Cut the bread into pieces and place in a food processor. Using the pulse button, blend the bread to make rough crumbs, as evenly sized as you can. Return the skillet/frying pan to a medium-high heat, add the breadcrumbs, and cook, stirring, for 5 minutes or until they are evenly golden and crisp. Combine with the bacon, parsley, and a little salt and pepper and set aside.

When the potatoes are tender, transfer half the soup to a liquidizer and blend until smooth. Return to the pan and stir. Taste and adjust the seasoning, then heat through.

Divide the soup between warm bowls and top with the pangrattato and a swirl of olive oil.

Smoked fish, bacon & charred corn chowder

A chowder is a fish soup made with a combination of stock, milk, and cream, traditionally thickened with crushed crackers or a roux. I prefer a slightly thinner version so I omit this part, resulting in a finished soup with a lighter and more modern feel. I love the depth of flavor provided by the smoked fish and the charred corn.

2 corn cobs, trimmed and husks discarded

1 tablespoon olive oil

1 lb. 2 oz./500 g smoked haddock or cod fillets

4 cups/900 ml chicken stock (see page 19) or vegetable stock

1¼ cups/300 ml whole/full-fat milk

2 sprigs of fresh thyme, bashed

2 bay leaves, bashed

9-oz./250-g piece of smoked bacon, rind removed, diced into ½-inch/1-cm cubes (or use thick slices/rashers or lardons)

1¾ tablespoons/25 g butter

1 onion, finely chopped

2 stalks/sticks of celery, thinly sliced

9 oz./250 g potatoes, diced into ½-inch/1-cm cubes

1 cup/250 ml light/single cream

a pinch of cayenne pepper

sea salt and freshly ground black pepper

2 tablespoons freshly snipped chives

SERVES 4

Preheat a griddle pan until hot. Rub the corn cobs with oil and season well with salt and pepper. Cook on the griddle pan for 5–8 minutes, turning frequently, until the kernels are charred and softened. Let cool, then cut down each side to remove the kernels. Discard the cobs and set the kernels aside.

Place the fish, stock, milk, and herbs in a skillet/frying pan over a medium heat. Bring to the boil and simmer gently for 5–6 minutes until the fish is just cooked through. Set aside to cool completely. Strain and reserve the cooled stock mixture. Discard the fish skin, flake the flesh into a bowl, and set aside.

Put the bacon into a 4-quart/litre Dutch oven and place over a low heat for 3–4 minutes until the fat is released. Then increase the heat to medium and fry for 4–5 minutes until the bacon is golden. Remove with a slotted spoon and set aside.

Add the butter to the pan and fry the onion and celery over a medium heat for 5 minutes until soft but not browned. Add the potatoes and cooled stock mixture and bring to the boil. Cover and simmer gently over a low heat for 10–15 minutes until the potatoes are tender.

Stir the flaked fish, charred corn, bacon, and cream into the Dutch oven and heat through for 3–4 minutes. Season to taste with salt and cayenne pepper. Divide the soup between warm bowls and serve garnished with the chives.

Chicken dumpling soup

This is a good old-fashioned chicken soup, thickened by the light and fluffy dumplings that add both bulk and extra flavor to the dish. It is particularly popular in the US, but variations of chicken dumpling soup can be found in countries as far and wide as Russia, Israel, and China, and across Europe.

3 tablespoons olive oil

2 leeks, trimmed and sliced

2 stalks/sticks of celery, sliced

2 carrots, finely chopped

2 tablespoons freshly chopped flat-leaf parsley

sea salt and freshly ground black pepper

CHICKEN STOCK

3¼ lb./1.5 kg free-range chicken

1 onion, roughly chopped

1 carrot, roughly chopped

1 stalk/stick of celery, roughly chopped

1 leek, thickly sliced

2 large garlic cloves, bashed

a sprig of fresh thyme, bashed

a sprig of fresh flat-leaf parsley, bashed

1 teaspoon sea salt

4 black peppercorns, bashed

DUMPLINGS

1 cup/125 g self-rising/raising flour

a pinch of salt

4 tablespoons/65 g butter, diced

3½ tablespoons/50 ml buttermilk

½ tablespoon wholegrain mustard

1 tablespoon freshly snipped chives

SERVES 6

Start by making the stock. Place the chicken in a 6-quart/litre Dutch oven with all the remaining stock ingredients and cover with cold water (about 3 quarts/litres). Bring the water slowly to the boil, skim the surface to remove any scum, and simmer gently, partially covered, for 1 hour. Remove the chicken from the stock and set aside to cool. Strain the stock through a fine strainer/sieve and measure 2½ quarts/litres back into the Dutch oven. If you have more liquid than this, reduce the liquid in the Dutch oven over a high heat until you have the right volume. Set the stock aside.

Once the chicken is cool, carefully peel away and discard the skin and bones. Reserve the dark meat for another dish. Finely shred the white meat and set aside.

Make the soup. Heat the oil in the same Dutch oven over a medium heat. Add the leeks, celery, and carrots, season with salt and pepper, and fry for 10 minutes until softened. Add the reserved chicken stock and bring to the boil. Cover the pan and simmer gently for 15 minutes until the carrots are tender. Stir in the shredded chicken and keep the soup warm.

Make the dumplings. Sift the flour into a bowl and stir in the salt. Rub in the butter until the mixture resembles fine breadcrumbs. Make a well in the middle, add the buttermilk, mustard, and chives, and bring the mixture together to form a firm dough. Shape the dough into 6 large or 12 small balls.

Place the dumpling balls in the broth and return to the boil. Cover the pan, reduce the heat, and simmer gently for 15 minutes until the dumplings are fluffed up and cooked through. Serve the soup in bowls scattered with the chopped parsley.

Roasted pumpkin soup with Parmesan & burnt sage butter

Pumpkin and sage are old friends and combine nowhere better than in this tasty soup. The pumpkin is roasted first (yes, in the Dutch oven) and then finished off in the stock with the remaining ingredients. Served drizzled with the sage butter and a good scattering of grated Parmesan, this soup is a real winner.

3¼ lb./1.5 kg pumpkin or butternut squash

3 tablespoons olive oil

2 sprigs of fresh sage

1 large onion, finely chopped

2 large garlic cloves, finely chopped

½ teaspoon smoked paprika

5 cups/1.25 litres hot chicken stock (see page 19) or vegetable stock

5 tablespoons/75 g butter

24 small sage leaves or 2 tablespoons chopped leaves

sea salt and freshly ground black pepper

SERVES 4

Preheat the oven to 400°F/180°C fan/200°C/Gas 6.

Peel and de-seed the pumpkin and cut the flesh into large chunks—you should have roughly 2¼–2¾ lb./1–1.2 kg flesh. Place the flesh in a 6-quart/litre Dutch oven and add 1 tablespoon of the oil, the sage sprigs, and a little salt and pepper and stir well. Transfer to the preheated oven and roast, uncovered, for 45 minutes, stirring halfway through, until tender and a little golden.

Meanwhile, heat the remaining oil in a medium skillet/frying pan and gently fry the onion and garlic with the smoked paprika and some salt and pepper for 10 minutes until really soft and lightly golden. Set aside until required.

Remove the Dutch oven from the oven and stir in the onion mixture and hot stock. Return to the oven, still uncovered, and cook for a further 15 minutes. Carefully remove from the oven and discard the sage. Purée the soup using an immersion/stick blender or liquidizer until smooth and season to taste.

Heat the butter and sage leaves together in a small saucepan over a medium heat for 2–3 minutes until the leaves are crisp and golden and the butter a nutty golden brown. Immediately remove the pan from the heat.

Divide the soup between warm bowls and spoon over the sage butter, including the leaves.

Mexican chicken & lime soup with avocado

This simple soup is a classic Mexican dish, with lime juice providing a lovely zingy freshness. Avocado is added at the end and this soup is typically served with a bowl of tortilla chips. If you can, always make your own chicken stock (see page 19)—it not only gives you a rich depth of nutritious flavor, but it also provides you with the chicken meat for this particular recipe.

3 tablespoons olive oil
1 onion, finely chopped
2 garlic cloves, finely chopped
1 green chile/chilli, seeded and chopped
grated zest of 1 lime
½ teaspoon ground coriander
¼ teaspoon ground cumin
1½ quarts/litres chicken stock (see page 19)
2 tomatoes, finely chopped
1 lb. 2 oz./500 g shredded cooked chicken (this will be the meat from the chicken cooked to make the stock)
freshly squeezed juice of 2 limes
1 avocado, peeled, pitted/stoned and chopped
a large handful of cilantro/coriander leaves, chopped
sea salt and freshly ground black pepper
tortilla chips, to serve

SERVES 4

Heat the oil in a 4-quart/litre Dutch oven over a medium heat. Fry the onion, garlic, chile/chilli, lime zest, spices, and some salt and pepper for 5–6 minutes until the onion is softened. Add the stock and tomatoes and bring to the boil, then reduce the heat and simmer gently for 10 minutes until the tomatoes are softened.

Stir in the chicken and lime juice and simmer for a further 5 minutes until the chicken is heated through.

Divide between soup bowls, top each one with the chopped avocado and cilantro/coriander leaves, and serve with a bowl of tortilla chips.

Spicy Korean noodle broth with kimchi

Kimchi is Korean pickled cabbage, a spicy accompaniment that is served with a wide range of dishes. I often make my own (see below) —it keeps for a long time and can be used in burgers, toasted sandwiches, soups, etc. Gochujang is a fermented Korean red chili/ chilli paste, available from specialist Asian stores or online.

1 lb. 2 oz./500 g boneless, skinless pork belly (or belly strips)

6 tablespoons dark soy sauce

1 tablespoon gochujang chili/chilli paste (see above), or regular chili/ chilli paste

½ tablespoon clear honey

1 teaspoon sesame oil

4 tablespoons/60 ml sake

4 tablespoons/60 ml mirin

4 eggs

2 tablespoons sunflower oil

5 cups/1.25 litres chicken stock (see page 19)

4 baby pak choi/bok choy, halved or sliced

4 scallions/spring onions, thinly sliced, plus extra to serve

10½ oz./300 g dried udon noodles

7 oz./200 g silken tofu, drained and diced

4 tablespoons kimchi (see right)

freshly ground black pepper

black sesame seeds, cilantro/ coriander leaves, and seaweed sprinkles, to serve

SERVES 4

Cut the pork belly into ¾-inch/2-cm cubes and place in a bowl. Add 1 tablespoon of the soy sauce, the chili/chilli paste, honey, sesame oil, and a little pepper and stir well until evenly coated. Set aside in a cool place to marinate for 1 hour (or longer, if wished). Combine the remaining soy sauce, sake, and mirin and set aside.

Cook the eggs in a saucepan of boiling water for 7 minutes. Remove from the pan and immediately plunge them into cold water. Let cool, peel, and cut in half. Cover with plastic wrap/clingfilm and set aside.

Heat the sunflower oil in a large skillet/frying pan over a medium high heat. Strain the marinated pork, reserving the juices. Add the pork to the pan and stir-fry for 5 minutes until golden brown. Remove with a slotted spoon and keep warm.

Pour the stock, soy mixture, and reserved marinade juices into a 2–3-quart/litre Dutch oven and bring to the boil. Reduce the heat and simmer, uncovered, for 5 minutes. Add the pak choi/bok choy and scallions/spring onions and cook for 2 minutes.

Meanwhile, cook the noodles in a saucepan of boiling water for 4 minutes. Drain, rinse well, drain again, and shake dry. Arrange the noodles in warm serving bowls and top each one with the pork, halved eggs, and tofu. Ladle over the hot broth and pak choi/bok choy and top each soup with a spoonful of kimchi. Serve garnished with sesame seeds, cilantro/coriander leaves, scallions/spring onions, and some seaweed sprinkles.

Quick kimchi: Place 12 oz./350 g shredded Chinese cabbage in a bowl and stir in 4 teaspoons salt and enough water to cover. Leave to soak for 30 minutes. Drain well and squeeze out excess water using a clean dish/tea towel. Place in a bowl with 2 thinly sliced scallions/spring onions. Mix together 2 tablespoons sugar, 1 tablespoon hot red pepper/ chilli flakes, 2 teaspoons grated root ginger, 2 crushed garlic cloves, 2 tablespoons fish sauce and 2 tablespoons sesame seeds to make a thin paste. Stir the paste into the cabbage, cover, and leave to marinate for 1 hour. Use as required. Store in a sealed jar in the fridge for up to 3 months.

Shrimp gumbo

Gumbo—the stew-like soup from the southern states of the US—is the official state cuisine of Louisiana. It includes the Holy Trinity of Creole ingredients—celery, red bell pepper, onions—and along with meat and seafood, it is thickened with okra.

2 lb. 4 oz./1 kg small raw unpeeled shrimp/prawns

5½ oz./150 g smoked bacon, rind removed and diced

1–2 tablespoons sunflower oil

1 lb. 2 oz./500 g okra, trimmed and thickly sliced

2 onions, finely chopped

1 red bell pepper, seeded and chopped

2 stalks/sticks of celery, finely chopped

4 garlic cloves, crushed

1 teaspoon freshly chopped thyme

1 teaspoon Creole spice mix (see right, or buy online)

14-oz/400-g can chopped tomatoes

2 bay leaves, bashed

sea salt and freshly ground black pepper

a handful of fresh cilantro/coriander, to serve

SERVES 6

Peel and de-vein the shrimp/prawns, reserving the heads and shells. Set the shrimp to one side. Rinse the heads and shells briefly under cold water, then place in a saucepan with 4 cups/1 litre cold water. Bring to the boil, skim the surface, and simmer gently for 30 minutes. Drain and discard the shells. Reserve 2 cups/500 ml of the cooking water (you can keep the rest and freeze for another dish).

Put the bacon in a 4-quart/litre Dutch oven and place over a medium heat. Allow the bacon to cook down to release its fat, then increase the heat to high and fry for 5 minutes until brown. Remove the bacon with a slotted spoon and set aside. Add a little oil to the pan if necessary, add the okra, and fry for about 5 minutes until lightly browned. Remove from the pan with the slotted spoon and set aside.

Add the remaining oil to the pan and fry the onions, bell pepper, celery, garlic, and some salt and pepper for 10 minutes until softened. Add the thyme and Creole spice mix and stir well. Cook for 1 minute, then stir in the tomatoes, reserved shrimp stock, bay leaves, and okra. Bring to the boil, then reduce the heat to low, cover, and simmer for at least 30 minutes, or until the okra is tender and the soup thickened.

Add the shrimp to the pan, stir well, and return the soup to the boil. Remove the pan from the heat but allow to sit undisturbed for 5 minutes until the shrimp are cooked. Adjust the seasoning, stir in the cilantro/coriander, and serve.

Creole spice mix: Combine 1 tablespoon each of onion powder, garlic powder, paprika, dried oregano, and dried basil and ½ tablespoon each of dried thyme, black pepper, white pepper, and cayenne pepper. Store in a screw-top jar, use as required.

Pea & ham soup with lemon & thyme oil

Pea and ham soup (also known as pease pudding) is made with dried split peas rather than fresh ones. A British favorite, this soup can be traced back to the Middle Ages when it was favored by sailors who added salt pork to the broth for extra protein and flavor. Still popular today, I like to add a swirl of zingy lemon and herb oil before serving, giving it a lovely freshness.

2 cups/400 g split green peas

1 onion, finely chopped

1 carrot, finely chopped

2 stalks/sticks of celery, finely chopped

2 garlic cloves, bashed

2 bay leaves, bashed

2 sprigs of fresh rosemary, bashed

12-oz./350-g piece of smoked bacon or pancetta, rind left on

sea salt and freshly ground black pepper

crusty bread, to serve

LEMON & THYME OIL

1 garlic clove

2 large sprigs of fresh thyme, plus extra to serve

grated zest of 1 lemon, plus extra to serve

7 tablespoons/100 ml extra virgin olive oil

SERVES 6

Rinse the split peas thoroughly under cold water and shake dry. Place in a 4-quart/litre Dutch oven with 2 quarts/litres cold water and bring to the boil. Simmer fast for 1 minute, removing any scum from the surface, then add all the remaining soup ingredients and bring to the boil. Reduce the heat, cover, and simmer for 1½–2 hours or until the peas are really tender. Season to taste (you may not need to add salt, as the bacon is already quite salty). Remove the bacon from the stock and cut away and discard the rind. Shred the meat, set aside, and keep warm.

Meanwhile, make the lemon and thyme oil. Place the garlic, thyme sprigs, and lemon zest in a mortar and pestle with a little salt and pound together to release the flavors and oils. Transfer to a small saucepan, pour over the olive oil, and heat very gently for 10 minutes without allowing it to come to a boil. Set aside to cool, then strain the oil, discarding the aromatics.

Divide the soup between warm bowls and top with the shredded bacon. Drizzle over the oil and serve with a little extra thyme, lemon zest, and freshly ground black pepper, plus crusty bread alongside.

Vietnamese chicken, rice & vinegar soup

Based on a Vietnamese dish called cháo gà which is served as a breakfast dish, this is a thick rice soup, almost like a savory porridge, packed full of flavor with chicken, herbs, spices, and aromatics. While I love this dish, I prefer it for dinner!

3¼ lb./1.5 kg free-range chicken

2 garlic cloves, crushed

2-inch/5-cm piece of root ginger, thickly sliced and bashed

6 makrut lime leaves, bashed

1–2 red chiles/chillies, lightly bashed

2 whole star anise, lightly bashed

⅓ cup/100 ml fish sauce

2 oz./50 g palm sugar, grated

freshly squeezed juice of 1 lime

1¾ cups/350 g short-grain rice

2 tablespoons rice wine vinegar

sea salt and freshly ground black pepper

sliced scallion/spring onion, cilantro/coriander leaves, crispy shallots, and chili/chilli oil, to serve

SERVES 6–8

Place the chicken in a 6-quart/litre Dutch oven and pour in enough water to completely cover the chicken (3–4 quarts/litres). Add the garlic, ginger, lime leaves, chiles/chillies, and star anise, plus a little salt and pepper.

Bring the water to the boil, skimming the surface of any scum as it starts to boil. Lower the heat and simmer, uncovered, for 1 hour. Carefully lift out the chicken and set aside to cool completely. Shred the meat into strips and discard the skin and bones.

Strain the broth through a fine strainer/sieve back into the pan and simmer until reduced to 2 quarts/litres. Add the fish sauce, palm sugar, and lime juice and stir to dissolve the sugar. Stir in the rice and return the broth to the boil. Simmer very gently, uncovered, for about 25–30 minutes until the rice is al dente. Stir in the shredded chicken and the vinegar and season to taste. Heat through for 5 minutes.

Divide between bowls and serve topped with sliced scallion/spring onion, cilantro/coriander leaves, crispy shallots, and chili/chilli oil.

Tip: The soup should be cooked and served straight away as the rice will continue to absorb the liquid, making it very thick and stodgy.

FISH & SEAFOOD

Shrimp paella

A Spanish-style paella can be cooked just as easily in a Dutch oven as in a traditional paella pan, despite the difference in the size and depth of the pans (although a wider pan is better suited). Using the heads and shells of the shrimp/prawns to enrich the stock is a sensible and resourceful way to use every part. Serve the paella with homemade aïoli (see below) as this adds extra richness to the finished dish.

6½ cups/1.5 litres fish stock or water

24 large raw shrimp/prawns, shells on

¼ teaspoon saffron strands

4 tablespoons/60 ml olive oil

1 small onion, finely chopped

4 garlic cloves, crushed

grated zest and freshly squeezed juice of 1 lemon

2 piquillo peppers from a jar, drained and finely chopped

2 tablespoons tomato paste/purée

1 teaspoon smoked paprika

1½ cups/300 g arborio rice

2 tablespoons freshly chopped flat-leaf parsley

sea salt and freshly ground black pepper

aïoli (see right) and lemon wedges, to serve

SERVES 4

Place the stock or water in a large saucepan (not your Dutch oven) Remove the heads and shells from the shrimp/prawns and add to the pan. Bring to the boil and simmer gently for 30 minutes, skimming any scum from the surface of the stock, then strain and discard the shells. Measure the liquid and pour 4 cups/1 litre. back into the saucepan, add the saffron strands, and set aside to infuse.

Take the peeled shrimp/prawns and cut down the back of each one with a sharp knife to reveal the intestinal tract within. Carefully pull it out and discard, then rinse and dry the shrimp. Set aside.

Heat the oil in a 4-quart/litre Dutch oven over a medium heat and fry the onion, garlic, and lemon zest for 10 minutes until softened. Add the chopped peppers, tomato paste/purée, and paprika and cook for a further 5 minutes until the sauce is quite dry. Add the rice, stir well for 1 minute, then pour in the reserved saffron-infused stock. Bring to the boil, then reduce the heat and simmer for 20 minutes or until almost all the liquid is absorbed. It should appear really quite thick and only a shallow layer of sauce will still be visible over the rice.

Stir the shrimp/prawns through the rice, cover the pan, and cook over a very low heat for a further 5 minutes. Remove the pan from the heat, but let sit undisturbed for a final 5 minutes. Stir the lemon juice through the pan. Serve scattered with parsley and lemon wedges and with a bowl of aïoli on the side.

Aïoli: Place 2 egg yolks, 2 teaspoons freshly squeezed lemon juice or white wine vinegar, 2 teaspoons Dijon mustard, and a little salt into a bowl and whisk until frothy. Very gradually add generous ¾ cup/200 ml olive oil (or a mixture of extra virgin olive oil and sunflower oil), whisking constantly until the sauce is thick and glossy. Season to taste.

Chinese-style braised fish with clams

One of the purest tasting and most sublime fish dishes I have ever eaten when cooked well, this steamed fish is a classic Chinese dish. Traditionally it is steamed in a bamboo steamer over simmering water, but the recipe can be adapted to work well in a Dutch oven. The clams add another delicious layer of flavor to the dish.

12 oz./350 g fresh vongole clams

1 lb. 2 oz.–1 lb. 7 oz./500–650 g whole snapper, bream, or bass, cleaned and scaled

2-inch/5-cm piece of root ginger, peeled

3 tablespoons Shaoxing rice wine

2 tablespoons light soy sauce

1 teaspoon granulated/caster sugar

½ teaspoon sesame oil

4 large scallions/spring onions, very thinly sliced

2 tablespoons peanut oil

cilantro/coriander leaves, to garnish

plain rice, to serve

SERVES 2

Wash the clams, then place in a large bowl, cover with cold water, and leave to soak for 1 hour. Drain, then rinse again and shake dry. Make 3–4 slashes into the flesh on both sides of the fish.

Heat an oval 4-quart/litre Dutch oven over a high heat, add the clams, cover, and cook for 3–4 minutes until all the shells have opened (discard any that remain closed). Strain the clam liquid into a measuring pitcher/jug and make up to 2 cups/500 ml with water if necessary. Set the clams to one side.

Allow the pan to cool completely, then line with a large piece of parchment paper. Cut the peeled ginger into thin slices and then into thin strips. Place the fish in the prepared pan, scatter over half the ginger, and pour in the clam stock and rice wine.

Cover the pan and bring to the boil, then lower the heat and simmer for 10 minutes. Remove the lid, scatter over the clams, cover again, and cook for a further 2 minutes or until the fish is cooked through and the clams reheated.

While the fish is cooking, combine the soy sauce, sugar, and sesame oil in a pitcher/jug. Place the peanut oil in a small saucepan and heat gently until the oil is shimmering hot.

Transfer the fish and clams to a warmed serving platter and drizzle over the soy sauce mixture. Top the fish with the remaining ginger and the scallions/spring onions, then immediately pour over the hot peanut oil. Sprinkle over the cilantro/coriander and serve with small bowls of plain rice.

Hot salmon kedgeree with cilantro & lime

Kedgeree is a dish of spiced rice, smoked fish, aromatics, fruit, and nuts that originated in India. Known there by many different names (kitcherie, kidgeree, khichuri, and, of course, kedgeree), its origins can be traced back to the 14th century. It was one of the many dishes favored by British settlers who introduced it as a breakfast dish during Victorian times, and has since become a favorite Anglo-Indian dish. My version uses whole salmon fillets, making it the perfect midweek supper.

4 large skinless salmon fillets, about 6½ oz./180 g each

8 slices of pancetta or smoked bacon rashers (rinds removed)

3 tablespoons sunflower oil

½ cup/50 g unsalted cashew nuts

1 onion, chopped

2 garlic cloves, crushed

1 teaspoon ground turmeric

½ teaspoon garam masala

1¾ cups/300 g long-grain rice

3¼ cups/750 ml chicken stock (see page 19)

6 whole cloves, lightly bashed

1 cinnamon stick, lightly bashed

⅓ cup/50 g raisins

1 tablespoon freshly chopped cilantro/coriander

freshly squeezed juice of 1 large lime

sea salt and freshly ground black pepper

aïoli (see page 34) or Greek yogurt, to serve (optional)

SERVES 4

Preheat the oven to 350°F/160°C fan/180°C/Gas 4.

Wrap each salmon fillet with 2 slices of the pancetta, criss-crossing them as you go and pressing them firmly in place. Heat the oil in a 4-quart/litre Dutch oven over a medium-high heat and fry the salmon for 1 minute on each side until the panceta is lightly golden. Remove from the pan and set aside.

Reduce the heat to medium, add the cashew nuts to the hot oil, and stir-fry for 1–2 minutes until golden, then remove with a slotted spoon and set aside.

Add the onion, garlic, and some salt and pepper to the pan and fry for 6–8 minutes until the onions are softened. Stir the turmeric, garam masala, and then the rice and cook over a low heat for 2 minutes. Pour in the stock, adding the cloves and cinnamon stick, and bring to a simmer. Cover the pan, transfer to the oven, and bake for 30 minutes.

Remove the pan from the oven and the lid from the pan. Stir the raisins, cashew nuts, cilantro/coriander, and lime juice through the rice and then arrange the salmon fillets on top, pressing down gently into the rice mixture. Cover the pan, return to the oven, and bake for a further 10 minutes until the salmon is cooked. Remove from the oven but let sit undisturbed for a final 5 minutes.

Divide the salmon and rice between plates and serve with some aïoli or Greek yogurt, if wished.

Sri Lankan fish curry

This is a lovely, deeply spiced fish curry from Sri Lanka. It uses fresh turmeric which you prepare in the same way as root ginger, by peeling and finely grating it. If you aren't able to find fresh turmeric, you can substitute 1 teaspoon ground turmeric.

1 lb. 10 oz./750 g skinless white fish fillets, such as bream, cod, or pollock

⅓ cup/80 ml tamarind juice

2 teaspoons ground cumin

2 teaspoons ground coriander

½ teaspoon chili/chilli powder

½ teaspoon sea salt

6 tablespoons/90 ml sunflower oil

2 onions, thinly sliced

a sprig of curry leaves, picked (optional)

1 cinnamon stick, lightly bashed

5 cardamom pods, lightly bashed

2 teaspoons freshly grated root ginger

4 garlic cloves, finely chopped

½-inch/1-cm piece of fresh turmeric, peeled and grated

2 medium tomatoes, finely chopped

1¼ cups/300 ml chicken (see page 19), fish, or vegetable stock

¾ cup/200 ml coconut milk, plus extra to serve

2 teaspoons granulated/caster sugar

freshly ground black pepper

cilantro/coriander leaves, to garnish

basmati rice, to serve

SERVES 4

Cut the fish fillets into ¾-inch/2-cm pieces. Mix the tamarind juice, cumin, coriander, chili/chilli powder, and salt into a paste. Place 2 tablespoons of the paste in a bowl with the fish pieces and stir well to lightly coat the pieces. Set aside until ready to cook.

Heat 2 tablespoons of the oil in a 2–3-quart/litre Dutch oven over a medium-high heat. Add about one third of the sliced onions and stir-fry for 8–10 minutes or until crisp and golden. Transfer to paper towels to drain and set aside.

Add another 2 tablespoons of the oil to the pan, add the curry leaves (if using), cinnamon stick, and cardamom pods, and cook for a few seconds until fragrant. Add the ginger, garlic, turmeric, and remaining onions and cook for 5–6 minutes, stirring constantly, until the onions are softened. Add the remaining paste mixture and fry for 1 minute, then stir in the tomatoes and cook for about 10 minutes until they soften and make a thick sauce. Add the stock, bring to a gentle simmer, cover and cook for 15 minutes. Stir in the coconut milk and sugar. Season to taste.

Heat the remaining oil in a large, non-stick skillet/frying pan over a high heat. Add the marinated fish in 2 batches and fry for 2–3 minutes until lightly browned. Spoon the fish and pan juices into the Dutch oven and simmer gently for 3 minutes until the fish is cooked through.

Divide between bowls and top with the crispy onions and cilantro/coriander leaves. Drizzle over a little extra coconut milk if wished and serve with some basmati rice on the side.

Oven-braised monkfish with salsa rossa

Monkfish is a meaty fish, and in this recipe it is treated in a similar way to a loin of meat in that it is stuffed, rolled up, and tied back together. Here the central bone from the tail is removed first, and the gap is stuffed before the two halves are reunited. Once tied into a roll, it is ready to bake on a bed of onion confit. It is served with a piquant tomato sauce, or salsa rossa.

2¾ lb./1.25 kg monkfish tail, skinned (or 2 x 1 lb. 7 oz./650 g tails)

a handful each of fresh sage, rosemary, and thyme

1 lemon, halved and thinly sliced

2 garlic cloves, thickly sliced

2 tablespoons olive oil

3½ tablespoons/50 g butter

3 red onions, thinly sliced

5 tablespoons/75 ml dry white wine

a few fresh basil leaves, to garnish (optional)

sea salt and freshly ground black pepper

SALSA ROSSA

3½ oz./100 g piquillo peppers from a jar, drained and chopped

1 tablespoon extra virgin olive oil

2 garlic cloves, crushed

2 large ripe tomatoes, roughly chopped

a small pinch of hot red pepper/chilli flakes

1 tablespoon dried oregano

1 tablespoon red wine vinegar

SERVES 4

Make the salsa rossa. Place the ingredients in a small saucepan, bring to the boil, then reduce the heat and simmer for 10–12 minutes or until thickened. Allow the sauce to cool, then purée it until smooth.

Preheat the oven to 400°F/180°C fan/200°C/Gas 6.

Carefully cut down each side of the monkfish bone and remove it without cutting the body completely in half (but don't worry if you do, as it ties back together). Pop the herbs, a few of the lemon slices, the garlic slices, and plenty of salt and pepper all the way along the gap. Tie together with string at 1-inch/2.5-cm intervals, keeping the aromatics in place.

Heat the oil in an oval 4–5-quart/litre Dutch oven and fry the fish for 3–4 minutes, turning, until well browned all over. Remove from the pan and set aside.

Add the butter to the pan and as soon as it has melted, add the onions. Stir over a medium heat for about 10 minutes or until starting to soften and turn translucent. Return the fish to the pan, arranging it over the onions, add the remaining lemon slices and the wine, bring to the boil, and cook for 2 minutes. Cover the pan, transfer to the preheated oven, and bake for 20–25 minutes until a skewer inserted into the center of the fish comes out hot. Remove from the oven, cover with foil, and leave to rest for 5 minutes before serving.

Remove the string and carve the monkfish into portions. Serve with the salsa rossa and a few basil leaves.

Tuscan seafood stew

A lavish, deeply flavored seafood stew typical of those you will find not only in Tuscany, but in slightly different guises all along the Italian coast. The mussel stock and shrimp/prawn heads, as well as red wine, provide a real depth of flavor and an amazing aroma. You need a total of 3¼–4½ lb./1.5–2 kg seafood, any mixture you like. The stew is served on a slice of chargrilled sourdough bread rubbed with garlic and extra virgin olive oil—sublime.

12 oz./350 g mussels or clams (or a mixture of both)

1¾–2 cups/400–500 ml fish stock

20 large raw shrimp/prawns, shells on

4 langoustines

9½ oz./250 g prepared squid bodies or rings

9½ oz./250 g firm fleshed fish fillets, such as swordfish

4 tablespoons/60 ml olive oil

1 large onion, finely chopped

4 garlic cloves, 3 crushed, 1 left whole

2 teaspoons freshly chopped thyme

1 teaspoon fennel seeds, toasted and crushed

1¼ cups/300 ml light red wine

1 lb. 10 oz./750 g ripe tomatoes, chopped

4 tablespoons tomato paste/purée

2 tablespoons freshly chopped basil or flat-leaf parsley

4 slices of ciabatta or sourdough bread

4 tablespoons/60 ml extra virgin olive oil

sea salt and freshly ground black pepper

SERVES 4

Prepare all the seafood. Scrub the mussels or clams, removing any scraggly bits or barnacles and rinse well. Place a 6-quart/litre Dutch oven over a high heat and when hot, add the mussels. Cover and cook for 3–4 minutes until the shells have opened (discard any that remain closed). Strain and reserve the stock (making it up to 2½ cups/600 ml with fish stock as necessary). Briefly refresh the mussels under cold water to prevent them cooking further. Set aside.

Taking the shrimp/prawns, snip a small slit into the back of each one through the shell to reveal the intestinal tract. Carefully pull this out and discard, rinse the shrimp/prawns and pat dry. Lay the langoustines on their backs and cut in half through the stomach, down between the legs and head. Scoop out and discard the intestines, rinse, and dry the langoustines. Cut the squid and fish fillet into bite-sized pieces.

Heat the olive oil in the same Dutch oven over a medium heat. Add the onion, crushed garlic, thyme, fennel seeds, and salt and pepper, and fry gently for 10 minutes until really softened. Add the wine and tomatoes and bring to the boil, then reduce the heat and simmer for 3–4 minutes until the alcohol is cooked off. Stir in the tomato paste/purée, then cover the pan and simmer for 20 minutes.

Stir the shrimp/prawns through the sauce, then lay the langoustines, squid, fish pieces, and finally the cooked mussels on top. Cover and cook for a further 5–6 minutes, then remove from the heat and let sit undisturbed for a final 5 minutes until all the seafood is cooked through. Season the sauce to taste and scatter over the basil or parsley.

Meanwhile, heat a ridged grill pan until hot and cook the bread slices for 1–2 minutes on each side until really nicely charred. Rub each one on both sides with the whole garlic clove and drizzle with the extra virgin olive oil. Place a slice of bread in the base of each serving bowl and spoon over the stew, making sure everyone gets an equal portion of all the seafood. Serve immediately.

Singapore chile crab stir-fry

Once again the Dutch oven shows its versatility as it makes the perfect pan for a stir-fry. As with a wok, it is important to get the pan hot before adding the oil, followed by the ingredients, to prevent them sticking to the pan. This crab dish is a true classic of Singaporean cuisine and is delicious, if a little messy—serve with bowls of lemon water and a bib!

2 lb. 4 oz./1 kg fresh crab, prepared (see tip)
1 bunch of scallions/spring onions
4 garlic cloves
1¼-inch/3-cm piece of root ginger, peeled and chopped
1 tablespoon shrimp paste
3 tablespoons peanut oil
14 oz./400 ml strained tomatoes/passata
2 tablespoons tomato paste/purée
2 tablespoons sweet chili/chilli sauce or chili/chilli jam
3 tablespoons light soy sauce
1 tablespoon kecap manis
cilantro/coriander leaves and sliced red chiles/chillies, to garnish
jasmine rice, to serve

SERVES 4

Wash and dry the prepared crab or crab claws and set aside.

Trim the ends from the scallions/spring onions and separate the white parts and the green parts. Roughly chop the white parts, then thinly slice the green parts for later. Place the chopped white scallions/spring onions, garlic, and ginger in a blender and purée to make a smooth paste, then stir in the shrimp paste.

Heat the oil in a 4-quart/litre capacity Dutch oven over a medium heat and fry the garlic paste for 3–4 minutes until fragrant. Add the strained tomatoes/passata, tomato paste/purée, sweet chili/chilli sauce or jam, soy sauce, and kecap manis and cook for 5 minutes until thickened.

Add the prepared crab, stir well, cover the pan, and simmer for 8–10 minutes until the crab is cooked through (or 6–8 minutes for precooked crab claws). Scatter over the green scallion/spring onion, cilantro/coriander, and sliced chiles/chillies, and serve with lime wedges. Accompany with jasmine rice.

Tip: It's best to use a live crab, so ask your fishmonger to kill the crab for you and ideally cut it up ready to stir-fry. Alternatively, use 2 lb. 4 oz./1 kg cooked crab claws, cracking the shells with a hammer and continuing as above.

Smoked fish pies with scallop potatoes

There is little better than a good fish pie. Here, the topping is scallop potatoes, rather than mashed potato or pastry, and it works really well. You can vary the fish if you like, but try to use some smoked fish as it adds a terrific depth of flavor.

- 7 tablespoons/100 g butter
- 2 leeks, thinly sliced
- 3 stalks/sticks of celery, thinly sliced
- ¼ cup/40 g all-purpose/plain flour
- 1½ cups/350 ml whole/full-fat milk
- ⅔ cup/150 ml single/light cream
- ½ cup/50 g mature cheese such as Cheddar or Monterey Jack, grated
- 7 oz./200 g frozen leaf spinach, thawed
- 9 oz./250 g skinless salmon fillet
- 9 oz./250 g smoked haddock fillet, skinned
- 5½ oz./150 g cooked peeled shrimp/prawns
- 1 lb. 10 oz./750 g potatoes, such as Yukon Gold, Russets, King Edwards, or Desiree
- sea salt and freshly ground black pepper
- green beans, to serve (optional)

SERVES 4

Preheat the oven to 375°F/170°C fan/190°C/Gas 5.

Melt half the butter in a skillet/frying pan over a medium heat and fry the leeks, celery, and a little salt and pepper for 10 minutes until soft but not browned. Stir in the flour and cook for a further 1 minute. Gradually add the milk and cream, stirring constantly, until the sauce is smooth. Bring to the boil, still stirring, and simmer gently for 2 minutes until thickened. Remove from the heat and stir in three-quarters of the grated cheese. Cover the entire surface with plastic wrap/clingfilm and set aside to cool.

Drain the spinach, squeeze out the excess water, then chop finely. Cut the salmon and smoked haddock into bite-sized pieces and cut the shrimp/prawns in half. Stir the spinach, fish, shrimp/prawns, and a little pepper into the leek sauce, then divide equally between 4 x 9-oz./250-ml individual Dutch ovens. Smooth flat.

Thinly slice the potatoes using either a mandolin or a very sharp knife. Melt the remaining butter and season with a little pepper. Arrange the potatoes in overlapping layers over the filling, brushing each layer with the melted butter. Finally, scatter over the remaining cheese.

Bake in the preheated oven for 30–35 minutes until the potatoes are golden and the filling bubbling. Serve with green beans, if wished.

Tip: You can use a 2–3-quart/litre Dutch oven rather than individual dishes if you wish. If so, cook for an extra 10–15 minutes until the topping is golden.

FISH & SEAFOOD 53

MEAT

Sicilian agrodolce-stuffed lamb

Sicily is a melting pot of culinary cultures, with influences from the east, north Africa, and the Mediterranean due to its geographical position. Many of its recipes combine ingredients from all these regions, as in this dish which includes herbs, spices, and aromatics. Agrodolce sauce is an Italian sweet-sour sauce—I am a real fan of sweet and savory in meat dishes, so this is a favorite of mine.

6 tablespoons/90 ml olive oil

2 garlic cloves, crushed

grated zest of 2 lemons

3½ oz./100 g day-old bread, crusts removed, made into breadcrumbs

scant ½ cup/50 g pine nuts, toasted and chopped

2 tablespoons freshly grated Pecorino or Parmesan

2 tablespoons freshly chopped mixed herbs, such as thyme and oregano

3¼ lb./1.5 kg boned lamb shoulder

sea salt and freshly ground black pepper

AGRODOLCE SAUCE

2 tablespoons extra virgin olive oil

1 small onion, finely chopped

1 small head of fennel, trimmed and chopped

2 garlic cloves, crushed

½ teaspoon ground cinnamon

1 lb. 2 oz./500 g ripe vine tomatoes, chopped

2 anchovies, drained and chopped

2 sprigs of fresh rosemary, bashed

scant ½ cup/50 g raisins

2 tablespoons capers, drained

2 tablespoons honey

1 tablespoon red wine vinegar

SERVES 4

Preheat the oven to 400°F/180°C fan/200°C/Gas 6.

Reserving 2 tablespoons of the oil, heat the remaining oil in a skillet/frying pan and gently fry the garlic and lemon zest over a low heat for 5 minutes until softened. Increase the heat to medium, add the breadcrumbs, and stir-fry for 2–3 minutes until coated with oil but not browned. Remove from the heat, stir in the pine nuts, Pecorino, and herbs, then season to taste. Allow to cool completely.

Open the boned lamb out flat and spread the stuffing down the center. Roll up as well as you can and, using kitchen string, tie the lamb up at ¾-inch/2-cm intervals to form a long roll. Season liberally with salt and pepper.

Heat the reserved olive oil in an oval 4-quart/litre Dutch oven over a high heat. Add the lamb and fry for 5–6 minutes, turning, until evenly browned. Remove from the pan.

Make the sauce. Add the oil to the same pan, reduce the heat, add the onion, fennel, and garlic and gently fry for 10 minutes until softened but not browned. Add the cinnamon, tomatoes, anchovies, rosemary, and a little salt and pepper. Return the lamb back to the pan and bring the sauce to a simmer. Cover, transfer the pan to the preheated oven, and cook for 1 hour.

Remove the pan from the oven and the lid from the pan. Take the lamb out and wrap it loosely in foil.

Stir the raisins, capers, honey, and vinegar into the pan and bring the sauce to a boil on the stovetop. Simmer for 10–15 minutes until the sauce is reduced and thickened.

Serve the lamb carved into thick slices with plenty of the agrodolce sauce alongside.

Greek-style lamb with orzo & dill

Orzo is a tiny rice-shaped pasta popular throughout the eastern Mediterranean, where it is also known as risoni. The Greek name for it is kritharaki and it is traditionally cooked with lamb in a rich tomato sauce in a terracotta pot on an open fire. It works well in the Dutch oven and can be cooked on the stovetop or in an oven, as here.

- 3¼ lb./1.5 kg lamb neck chops (allow 2–3 per person)
- 4 tablespoons/60 ml olive oil
- 1 large onion, sliced
- 2 carrots, chopped
- 2 large garlic cloves, finely chopped
- ⅔ cup/150 ml red wine
- 14-oz/400-g can chopped tomatoes
- 3¼ cups/750 ml chicken stock (see page 19)
- 1 teaspoon fennel seeds, toasted and roughly crushed
- 2 teaspoons dried oregano
- 2 teaspoons ground allspice
- 7 oz./200 g orzo or small soup pasta
- 2 tablespoons freshly chopped dill
- sea salt and freshly ground black pepper

SERVES 4

Preheat the oven to 325°F/140°C fan/160°C/Gas 3.

Season the lamb chops with salt and pepper. Heat 1 tablespoon of the oil in a 5–6-quart/litre Dutch oven over a high heat. Add the chops and fry for 5 minutes on each side until evenly browned. Remove from the pan with a slotted spoon and reduce the heat to medium.

Add the remaining oil to the pan, then add the onion, carrots, and garlic, season with salt and pepper, and fry gently for 10 minutes until the onion is softened. Return the lamb to the pan. Add the wine and simmer for 2–3 minutes, then stir in the tomatoes, stock, fennel seeds, oregano, and allspice. Bring to the boil, cover the pan, and transfer to the preheated oven. Bake for 1½–2 hours, until the meat is tender.

Remove the pan from the oven and the lid from the pan. Stir in the orzo, cover, and return the pan to the oven for a further 10–15 minutes until the pasta is cooked. Scatter over the dill and let sit for 5 minutes before serving.

Whole leg of lamb pilaff

My favorite part of this recipe is that you use all the delicious pan juices that ooze from the meat as it roasts to then cook the rice while the lamb rests. The dish is served with an equally delicious fresh Indian-style relish of pomegranate seeds, herbs, and lime juice. Start this recipe a day ahead.

3¼ lb./1.5 kg leg of lamb (bone-in weight)

1 tablespoon coriander seeds

2 teaspoons cumin seeds

2 teaspoons fennel seeds

8 cardamom pods, seeds only

1 whole star anise

¼ teaspoon black peppercorns

4 garlic cloves, crushed

2-inch/5-cm piece of root ginger, peeled and grated

1¼ cups/250 ml natural yogurt

2 teaspoons granulated/caster sugar

freshly squeezed juice of ½ lemon

1 teaspoon sea salt

1 large onion, thinly sliced

1 cinnamon stick, bashed

1¾ cups/350 g basmati rice

a small pinch saffron strands

sea salt and freshly ground black pepper

your favorite curry chutney, to serve (optional)

POMEGRANATE RELISH

1 small red onion, finely chopped

½ bunch of fresh mint leaves, torn

½ bunch of fresh cilantro/coriander leaves, picked

seeds of 1 pomegranate

freshly squeezed juice of 1 large lime

2 teaspoons clear honey

SERVES 6

A day ahead, make several slashes into the flesh all over the lamb. Set aside. Heat a dry skillet/frying pan over a medium heat, add the whole spices (but not the cinnamon stick), and cook, stirring, for 3–4 minutes or until they are aromatic and starting to brown. Set aside to cool, then grind the spices to a fine powder using a spice grinder (or a mortar and pestle). Combine the ground spices, garlic, ginger, yogurt, sugar, lemon juice, and salt in a bowl. Spread or spoon the yogurt mixture all over the lamb and place it in a large ceramic dish. Cover the whole dish with plastic wrap/clingfilm and leave to marinate for 12 hours in the fridge.

The next day, remove the lamb from the fridge 1 hour before cooking. Preheat the oven to 300°F/130°C fan/150°C/Gas 2.

Place the onion in a 6–8-quart/litre Dutch oven (see Tip, below) and lay the lamb and all the marinade on top. Add ⅔ cup/150 ml warm water and the cinnamon stick, cover the pan, and transfer to the preheated oven. Roast for 3 hours or until the lamb is really tender. Remove the lid and cook for a further 15 minutes to brown the crust a little.

Remove the lamb from the pan, cover with foil, and keep warm. Carefully strain the juices into a measuring pitcher/jug (discarding the onions and cinnamon) and if necessary make the juices up to 2 cups/500 ml with water. Return the juices to the pan and stir in the rice. Scatter the saffron over the top and bring to the boil on the stovetop. Reduce the heat to low, cover the pan, and cook for 15 minutes. Turn off the heat, but leave for a further 10 minutes until the rice is tender.

Meanwhile, make the relish. Place all the ingredients in a bowl and stir well. Carve the lamb into thick slices and serve with the rice and the pomegranate relish.

Tip: I recommend using a large oval Dutch oven with at least an 8-quart/litre capacity to be sure your leg of lamb fits in. Alternatively, if your Dutch oven is smaller, ask your butcher to trim the end of the leg, cutting through the bone so that it fits.

Moroccan lamb with dates & olives

This recipe is another great example of mixing food cultures and ingredients together to produce a rich and deeply flavorful dish. Based on a classic Moroccan tagine, red wine is an unusual addition but it helps to tenderize the lamb. Start this recipe a day ahead.

6 small lamb shanks (or lamb neck chops), about 3¼ lb./1.5 kg in total

2 onions, roughly chopped

2 red bell peppers, seeded and roughly chopped

4 garlic cloves, chopped

4 sprigs of fresh rosemary, bashed

1 orange, thickly sliced

2 cinnamon sticks, bashed

750-ml bottle red wine

2 tablespoons olive oil

1 tablespoon ras el hanout (see below)

14-oz/400-g can chopped tomatoes

2 tablespoons date syrup or molasses

4½ oz./125 g small pitted black olives

2½ oz./75 g dates, pitted and chopped

4 tablespoons freshly chopped cilantro/coriander

sea salt and freshly ground black pepper

couscous, cilantro/coriander, and pomegranate seeds, to serve

RAS EL HANOUT

3 cardamom pods, seeds only

1 teaspoon coriander seeds

½ teaspoon cumin seeds

½ teaspoon sweet paprika

½ teaspoon ground cinnamon

½ teaspoon ground cayenne

½ teaspoons ground turmeric

½ teaspoon ground ginger

SERVES 6

A day ahead, place the lamb shanks in a large ceramic bowl or plastic container. Add the onions, peppers, garlic, rosemary, orange slices, cinnamon sticks, and some salt and pepper. Pour over the wine and leave to marinate overnight in the fridge.

Make the ras el hanout. Place the cardamom seeds, coriander seeds, and cumin seeds in a small dry skillet/frying pan and place over a medium heat. Cook for 2–3 minutes until they are browned and starting to release their aroma. Allow to cool and then grind to a fine powder in a spice grinder (or use a mortar and pestle). Mix with the powdered spices and store in a jar until required.

The next day, strain the marinade juices into a pitcher/jug, reserving all the vegetables and set both aside. Pat the lamb shanks dry with paper towels and season generously with salt and pepper.

Heat half the oil in a 6-quart/litre Dutch oven over a high heat. Fry the shanks for 5 minutes until browned all over. Remove with a slotted spoon and reduce the heat to medium. Add the remaining oil and the reserved vegetables to the pan (but not the orange slices) and fry for 5–6 minutes over a medium heat until browned and sticky. Stir in the ras el hanout spice mix, stir for 1 minute.

Return the lamb to the pan with the orange slices, the marinade juices, tomatoes, and date syrup, stirring well. Bring the stew to the boil, cover, reduce the heat, and simmer over a very low heat for 2 hours until the lamb is starting to fall from the bone. Remove the lid, stir in the olives and dates and cook uncovered for a further 15 minutes until the sauce has thickened. Stir in the cilantro/coriander and adjust seasoning to taste.

Serve with the couscous, herbs, and pomegranate seeds.

Vietnamese-style miso, red wine & caramel beef cheeks

Many Vietnamese dishes pair meat or fish with a sweet caramel sauce to balance the saltiness of fish sauce, the fire of chiles/chillies, and the sharpness of lime juice—the main flavors we associate with south-east Asian cooking. Add in Japanese miso and red wine, and you have a truly global dish. Beef cheeks need a long cooking time before they soften to mouthwatering tenderness.

3¼ lb./1.5 kg beef cheeks
2 cups/500 ml beef stock
2 cups/500 ml red wine
1¼ cups/250 g granulated/caster sugar
4 tablespoons brown miso paste
4 tablespoons/60 ml fish sauce
1 tablespoon light soy sauce
4 garlic cloves, bashed
2-inch/5-cm piece of root ginger, peeled and bashed
2 whole star anise, lightly bruised
2 cinnamon sticks, lightly bruised
jasmine rice, to serve

PICKLES

2 tablespoons freshly squeezed lime juice
1 tablespoon fish sauce
1 tablespoon sugar
2 carrots, trimmed and thinly sliced
1 zucchini/courgette, trimmed and thinly sliced
½ cucumber, seeded and thinly sliced
a few fresh mint and cilantro/coriander leaves
1 red chile/chilli, sliced (optional)

SERVES 8

Preheat the oven to 300°F/130°C fan/150°C/Gas 2.

Wash and dry the beef cheeks and then cut into 2-inch/5-cm pieces. Place in a 4–5-quart/litre Dutch oven, cover with cold water, bring to the boil, and cook for 5 minutes, skimming all the scum from the surface. Drain and discard the water, wipe the pan clean, and return the beef to the pan. Add the stock and wine to the pan and bring to the boil.

Meanwhile, place the sugar in a small saucepan ½ cup/125 ml water. Bring to the boil and simmer for 8–10 minutes without stirring, until the liquid starts to caramelize and turn a golden brown. Immediately stir the caramel sauce into the stock.

Combine the miso, fish sauce, and soy sauce until smooth and stir into the pan with the garlic, ginger, star anise, and cinnamon sticks. Return to the boil and place a sheet of parchment paper over the surface of the stew. Cover the pan with the lid and transfer to the preheated oven. Cook for 4–5 hours, checking after 4 hours to see how the meat is cooking—it should be falling apart and the juices should be starting to thicken.

About 30 minutes before the beef is ready, make the vegetable pickles. Combine the lime juice, fish sauce, and sugar, stirring to dissolve the sugar. Combine the sliced vegetables in a bowl, pour the lime mixture over the top, and stir well. Add the herbs and chile/chilli.

Using a slotted spoon, transfer the beef cheeks to a warmed platter. Place the pan on the stovetop, bring the pan juices to a simmer and cook for 5 minutes until the sauce is glossy and thickened. Pour the meat juices over the beef cheeks and serve with the pickles and some jasmine rice.

Oven-baked meatballs with cheesy tomato sauce

This is an all-round winner. Tasty meatballs, a rich tomato ragù, a little cream for extra comfort, and a layer of meltingly gooey mozzarella all combine to make a type of meatball lasagne! A great midweek dinner for the family—kids will love this one.

1 lb./450 g ground/minced beef

10½ oz./300 g ground/minced pork

1 small onion, very finely chopped

2 teaspoons English mustard

2 teaspoons freshly chopped thyme

2 tablespoons olive oil

2 x 14-oz/400-g cans chopped tomatoes

4 garlic cloves, crushed

1 teaspoon granulated/caster sugar

a pinch of hot red pepper/chilli flakes

4 tablespoons freshly chopped basil, plus extra to garnish

5 tablespoons/75 ml light/single cream

7 oz./200 g mozzarella cheese, sliced

sea salt and freshly ground black pepper

pasta or bread and a crisp green salad, to serve

SERVES 4–6

Combine the beef, pork, onion, mustard, thyme, and plenty of salt and pepper in a bowl. Mix this together with your hands to form a really good sticky mixture. Then, using slightly damp hands, shape into 20–24 golfball-sized meatballs. Cover and let sit in a cool place for 1 hour.

Preheat the oven to 325°F/140°C fan/160°C/Gas 3.

Heat the oil in a 4-quart/litre Dutch oven, add the meatballs, and cook in batches, for 3–4 minutes until evenly browned. Remove with a slotted spoon. Add the tomatoes, garlic, 1 teaspoon sea salt, sugar, hot red pepper/chilli flakes, and basil to the pan and bring to the boil. Pop the meatballs into the sauce, cover, and transfer the pan to the preheated oven. Cook for 1 hour or until the sauce is thick and glossy and the meatballs cooked through.

Remove the pan from the oven and the lid from the pan. Very carefully pour the cream around the meatballs and then lay the mozzarella slices on top. Return to the oven, uncovered, and cook for a further 10–15 minutes until the cheese is melted.

Scatter with some fresh basil leaves and serve with some pasta or bread and a crisp green salad.

Beef short rib daube with persillade

Daube of beef is a Provençal stew traditionally cooked in a daubière, a terracotta pot made by local artisans. Luckily our Dutch oven makes a great substitute. I like to use short beef ribs rather than the more normal brisket or chuck steak, as I find the combination of the meat, fat, and small bones imparts a wonderful flavor to the stew. The persillade—a combination of freshly chopped parsley, garlic, lemon zest, and vinegar—cuts through the richness of the dish, adding a delightful finish. Start this recipe a day ahead.

4½ lb./2 kg short beef ribs

7 tablespoons/100 ml olive oil

5½-oz./150-g piece of pancetta, rind removed, diced

9 oz./250 g button mushrooms

2 onions, chopped

2 carrots, chopped

2 garlic cloves, chopped

2 sprigs of fresh thyme

1 sprig of fresh rosemary

grated zest and freshly squeezed juice of 1 orange

4 tablespoons tomato paste/purée

750-ml bottle rich and fruity red wine

2 cups/500 ml beef stock

⅓ cup/30 g pitted black olives

sea salt and freshly ground black pepper

creamed polenta and green beans, to serve

PERSILLADE

4 tablespoons freshly chopped flat-leaf parsley

½ small garlic clove, crushed

grated zest of 1 lemon

1–2 teaspoons white wine vinegar

SERVES 6

Starting a day ahead, preheat the oven to 325°F/140°C fan/160°C/Gas 3.

Season the beef ribs liberally with salt and pepper. Heat 1 tablespoon of the oil in a 6–8-quart/litre Dutch oven over a medium-high heat and fry the ribs, in batches, for 10 minutes, turning regularly until evenly browned. Set aside. Wipe the pan clean, discarding the fat.

Add 2 tablespoons of the oil to the pan and once hot, fry the pancetta for 5 minutes until golden, then remove with a slotted spoon and add to the beef. Add 2 more tablespoons of oil, increase the heat, and fry the mushrooms for 3–4 minutes until browned. Remove with a slotted spoon, cool, and chill until required.

Reduce the heat to low. Add the remaining oil to the pan and fry the onions, carrots, garlic, and herbs with a little salt and pepper for 10 minutes until softened. Stir in the orange zest and tomato paste/purée and stir for 1 minute, then add the wine, stock, orange juice, beef ribs, and pancetta. Bring to the boil, cover with the lid, and transfer to the preheated oven. Cook for 3–3½ hours or until the meat is falling from the bones, checking from time to time for doneness. Remove from the oven and allow to cool completely, then chill in the fridge overnight.

The next day, remove as much of the fat from the top of the stew as you can and place the pan on the stovetop. Bring slowly to the boil, add the mushrooms and olives, and cook gently for 15 minutes until the meat is heated through.

To make the persillade, stir all the ingredients together in a bowl.

Serve the beef stew topped with a little persillade, on a bed of creamy polenta and with some green beans.

Hungarian goulash with cornbread dumplings

A classic Hungarian stew topped with savory cornbread dumplings makes this a complete one-pot meal. The richness of the sauce is enhanced by the paprika. Although sweet paprika is more traditional, I love to use smoked for extra flavor—you can choose whichever you prefer.

6 tablespoons/90 ml olive oil

3¼ lb./1.5 kg braising or chuck steak, cubed into ¾-inch/ 2-cm pieces

2 onions, thinly sliced

2 red bell peppers, seeded and roughly chopped

2 garlic cloves, finely chopped

1 tablespoon sweet or smoked paprika, plus extra to dust

2 teaspoons caraway seeds

5 cups/1.25 litres beef or chicken stock (see page 19)

4 tablespoons tomato paste/purée

sea salt and freshly ground black pepper

sour cream or crème fraîche, to serve

CORNBREAD DUMPLINGS

1 cup plus 2 tablespoons/ 150 g all-purpose/plain flour

1 tablespoon baking powder

a pinch cayenne pepper

1 cup/150 g instant cornmeal/ polenta

½ cup/50 g finely grated Cheddar

1 tablespoon freshly chopped flat-leaf parsley

1 cup/250 ml buttermilk

SERVES 4–6

Preheat the oven to 350°F/160°C fan/180°C/Gas 4.

Heat half the oil in a 5–6-quart/litre Dutch oven and fry the beef, in batches, for 5 minutes until browned on all sides. Remove from the pan with a slotted spoon. Add the remaining oil and fry the onions, bell peppers, and garlic for 5 minutes, then stir in the paprika, caraway seeds, and a little salt and pepper, and fry for a further 5 minutes until the onions and peppers are softened.

Return the beef to the pan, add the stock and tomato paste/purée, stirring well, and bring to the boil. Cover the pan and transfer it to the preheated oven. Bake for 2 hours (or until the beef is tender).

Make the dumplings. Sift the flour, baking powder, and cayenne pepper into a bowl and stir in the polenta, cheese, parsley, and a little salt and pepper. Make a well in the middle and add the buttermilk. Work together to make a soft dough.

Remove the pan from the oven and the lid from the pan. Carefully spoon in 12 dollops of the dumpling mixture to cover the meat (but leave gaps in between each one). Cover with the lid and return the pan to the oven. Cook for 15–20 minutes or until the dumplings are puffed up. Check they are cooked by inserting a skewer into the middle—it should come out clean; if not, cook for a further 5 minutes until ready.

Serve the goulash accompanied by some sour cream or crème fraîche and a dusting of paprika, if wished.

Rolled pork belly in cider with crispy crackling

Allowing the pork skin to dry out in the fridge before cooking helps to crisp the skin up beautifully. After a quick sear in a very hot pan to aid the crisping process, the pork is then roasted in the stock, cider, and milk until tender. Start this recipe up to 48 hours before cooking.

4½ lb./2 kg boneless pork belly, skin on

2 tablespoons olive oil

12 small shallots, peeled but left whole

3 large carrots, roughly chopped

3 leeks, thickly sliced

1 head of garlic, cut in half

2–3 sprigs of fresh sage

2 bay leaves, bashed

1¼ cups/300 ml hard cider

1¼ cups/300 ml chicken stock (see page 19)

1¼ cups/300 ml milk

sea salt and freshly ground black pepper

SERVES 6

At least 24 and up to 48 hours before cooking, unwrap the pork belly and place, skin side up, on a plate. Pop uncovered into the fridge to dry out thoroughly until required, remembering to remove it from the fridge 1 hour before cooking.

The day of cooking, preheat the oven to 350°F/160°C fan/180°C/Gas 4.

Using a sharp knife, carefully slice between the pork skin and the layer of fat and remove the skin in one piece (you can ask your butcher to do this for you if you prefer). Season the fat layer, then return the skin and carefully roll up the whole belly. Tie at ¾-inch/2-cm intervals with kitchen string. Rub the skin with a good sprinkling of salt and pepper.

Heat the oil in a large skillet/frying pan over a medium heat. Add the pork and cook for 8–10 minutes, turning occasionally, until the skin is golden brown and crispy. Remove from the pan.

Arrange the vegetables, garlic halves, sage sprigs, and bay leaves in an oval 6-quart/litre Dutch oven and place the pork on top. Pour the cider, stock, and milk around the pork, cover, and transfer the pan to the preheated oven. Cook for 1½ hours until the meat is tender.

Increase the oven temperature to 450°F/210°C fan/230°C/Gas 8 and line a baking sheet with parchment paper. Remove the pan from the oven. Carefully lift the pork out onto a warm plate and snip away the string. Place the skin on the prepared baking sheet and return it to the oven for 10 minutes or so until it is really crisp.

Meanwhile, using a slotted spoon, transfer the vegetables to the pork platter, cover loosely with foil, and keep warm. Spoon away as much of the layer of fat from the top of the sauce as you can and bring the pan juices to the boil on the stovetop. Simmer for 3–4 minutes or until thickened.

Carve the pork into slices and the skin into strips, and serve with the vegetables and gravy.

Slow-cooked pork carnitas tacos

This is a Mexican dish—carnitas means "little meats," referring to the strips of pork that pull apart with a fork thanks to the long, slow cooking process. For this reason it is also called pulled pork. Carnitas are served with an array of accompaniments to choose from and wrapped up in corn tortillas. Start this recipe a day ahead.

1 head of garlic, cloves separated but left unpeeled
1 tablespoon sea salt
1 tablespoon dried oregano
2 teaspoons ground cinnamon
1 teaspoon ground cumin
freshly squeezed juice of 2 limes
2 lb. 4 oz./1 kg piece of boneless pork shoulder
freshly squeezed juice of 1 orange
2 tablespoons olive oil
2 bay leaves, bashed
freshly ground black pepper

RED ONION PICKLE
½ cup/125 ml cider vinegar
1 teaspoon sea salt
1 tablespoon granulated/caster sugar
2 small red onions, thinly sliced

TO SERVE
8 small corn tortillas
2 tomatoes, finely chopped
a handful of fresh cilantro/coriander leaves
arugula/rocket
chili/chilli sauce
lime wedges
mayonnaise

SERVES 4

A day ahead, heat a 4-quart/litre Dutch oven over a medium heat. Add the garlic cloves and cook for about 10 minutes, turning frequently, until the skins have blackened. Set aside to cool completely, then discard the skins.

Place the garlic in a mortar and pestle (or a food processor) with the salt and pound until well crushed. Add the oregano, spices, and the lime juice and work to a paste. Place the pork in a ceramic dish, add the paste, and rub well into the meat. Cover and refrigerate overnight.

The next day, return the pork to room temperature 1 hour before cooking. Preheat the oven to 300°F/130°C fan/150°C/Gas 2.

Remove the pork, discarding the marinade, and wash the pork under cold water. Pat dry on paper towels. Place the pork in the Dutch oven and add the orange juice, half the olive oil, bay leaves, and pepper. Cover the pan, transfer to the preheated oven, and cook for 3–4 hours (check from 2 hours onwards) until the meat is falling apart. Remove from the oven, but leave undisturbed for 30 minutes.

Meanwhile, make the red onion pickle. Place the vinegar, salt, and sugar in a saucepan and heat gently until the sugar is dissolved. Place the onion slices in a bowl and immediately pour over the pickling vinegar. Leave to go cold.

Remove the rested pork from the pan and reserve 2–3 tablesoons of the juices. Wash and dry the pan. Heat the remaining oil in the pan until really hot. Add the pork and brown over a high heat for 2–3 minutes on each side until the coloring is even and crisp. Using 2 forks, shred the meat, adding the reserved cooking juices. Remove from the heat, cover, and keep warm.

Heat the tortillas in a preheated skillet/frying pan or griddle pan, keeping them warm in a dish towel until they are all heated through. To serve, arrange all the parts on a table—pulled pork, tortillas, red onion pickle, chopped tomatoes, cilantro/coriander leaves, arugula/rocket, chili/chilli sauce, lime wedges, and mayonnaise. Allow guests to serve themselves and create their own wraps.

Slow roasted pork ribs with cabbage & apple slaw

A large part of American food culture revolves around the barbecue and pork rib racks are an integral part of this, and rightly so—there is little better than chewing on a sticky, tender, and lip-smacking pork rib. I wasn't sure how this classic dish would work in a Dutch oven, but I am really delighted with the result—after a long, slow braise, the ribs are returned to the Dutch oven, brushed with the glaze, and cooked on a high heat in the oven. Perfect.

4½ lb./2 kg pork rib racks
1 cup/250 ml hard cider
²/₃ cup/150 ml pineapple juice
¼ cup/75 ml clear honey
4 tablespoons tomato paste/purée
1 teaspoon ground cinnamon
1 teaspoon smoked paprika
½ teaspoon ground allspice
1 teaspoon sea salt
fries, to serve

CABBAGE & APPLE SLAW
1 teaspoon fennel seeds
¼ green cabbage, shredded
1 small onion, very thinly sliced
1 apple, skin on, cored, quartered, and cut into thin batons
¼ teaspoon sugar
¼ teaspoon sea salt
2 teaspoon freshly squeezed lime juice
4 tablespoons mayonnaise

SERVES 4

Preheat the oven to 300°F/130°C fan/150°C/Gas 2. Line an 8-quart/litre Dutch oven with a large sheet of parchment paper so the paper comes a little way up the sides of the pan.

Cut the rib racks into 4 portions and pop them into the prepared pan. Stir the remaining ingredients together well in a pitcher/jug, then pour over the ribs. Top with a second layer of parchment paper, cover the pan with a tight fitting lid, and transfer to the preheated oven. Cook for 3–4 hours, checking after 2½ hours and keeping an eye on the ribs until you see the meat starting to loosen from the bones.

Meanwhile, make the slaw. Place the fennel seeds and vegetables in a bowl. Add the sugar, salt, and lime juice and stir until really well mixed. Set aside for 10 minutes. Stir in the mayonnaise and set aside.

Remove the pan from the oven and the lid from the pan. Increase the oven temperature to 450°F/210°C fan/230°C/Gas 8.

Transfer the ribs (discarding the paper) to a large platter and strain the juices into a small saucepan. Bring to the boil and simmer for 5–6 minutes until the sauce is thick and glossy.

If necessary wash the pan and dry well. Line the pan with another large sheet of parchment paper and return the ribs to the pan. Pour the sauce over the top and return to the oven. Cook for 10–15 minutes, turning and glazing halfway through until the ribs are sticky with the glaze. Allow to cool for 10 minutes, then serve the ribs with the slaw and fries.

Boston baked beans

The original recipe for baked beans dates back to the early days of American food culture. Beans were a staple food of native Americans, who cooked them in a sauce and ate them with a type of cornbread. It is thought that early Dutch settlers, arriving into Boston, brought their braadpans (Dutch ovens) with them and these great cooking pots soon found their way into American kitchens. This is generally considered to be how this dish got its name, and today it is certainly synonymous with the dish of rich beans in a sauce with meat and molasses cooked in Dutch oven. Start this recipe a day ahead.

2 cups/350 g dried navy/haricot beans
1 lb. 2 oz/ 500 g gammon knuckle
½ teaspoon baking soda/bicarbonate of soda
1 garlic clove, crushed
1 onion, finely chopped
2 cups/500 ml strained tomatoes/passata
2 tablespoons tomato paste/purée
⅓ cup/125 g molasses or black treacle
1 tablespoon Dijon mustard
1 tablespoon red wine vinegar
a few drops of Tabasco sauce
sea salt and freshly ground black pepper
toasted bread, to serve
freshly chopped flat-leaf parsley (optional)

SERVES 4–6

A day ahead, place the beans in a large bowl and cover with cold water. Place the gammon in a second bowl (or large pan) and cover with cold water. Leave both to soak overnight. The next day, drain them both.

Preheat the oven to 300°F/130°C fan/150°C/Gas 2.

Place the beans in a 6-quart/litre Dutch oven and add enough water to cover them by a good 4 inches/10 cm. Add the baking soda/bicarbonate of soda and bring to a rolling boil. Cook fast for 10 minutes, then strain the beans and reserve 3 cups/750 ml of the cooking liquid.

Return the drained beans and the reserved liquid to the Dutch oven and add all the remaining ingredients, including the gammon, plus a little salt and pepper. Bring to the boil, cover, and transfer the pan to the preheated oven. Bake for 2½ hours, then check the level of the liquid, add a little more if the dish is dry, and continue to cook for a further 30 minutes until the beans and gammon are tender.

Carefully remove the skin, bone, and fat from the gammon and as soon as you can, shred the meat. Season the beans to taste with a little more salt and pepper. Serve the beans and shredded gammon with toasted bread, scattered with a little parsley, if wished.

POULTRY

Cajun chicken & seafood jambalaya

The Cajun version of jambalaya, a rice dish similar to paella, combines some type of meat with seafood. It hails from the low-lying swamp region of Louisiana where shrimp, crayfish, and even alligators are in abundance; add in some smoked sausage and you have your classic dish. The main difference between a Cajun and a Creole jambalaya is that the former is brown from the mixed spice mixture and the latter, red from the addition of canned tomatoes.

3–4 tablespoons olive oil

4 chicken thigh pieces, about 1 lb. 2 oz./500 g in total

1 medium andouille or smoked pork sausage, thickly sliced

1 onion, finely chopped

1 stalk/stick of celery, finely chopped

1 green bell pepper, seeded and chopped

2 garlic cloves, crushed

1 bay leaf

1½ cups/250 g long-grain rice

2½ cups/600 ml chicken stock (see page 19)

9 oz./250 g small raw shrimp/prawns, peeled and deveined

2 tablespoons freshly chopped cilantro/coriander

lemon wedges, to serve

sea salt and freshly ground black pepper

CAJUN SPICE MIX

1 teaspoon black peppercorns, ground

1 teaspoon sweet paprika

1 teaspoon onion powder

½ teaspoon garlic powder

½ teaspoon dried oregano

¼ teaspoon dried thyme

¼ teaspoon cayenne pepper

SERVES 4

To make the spice mix, simply combine all the spices in a small bowl.

Heat the oil in a 2-quart/litre Dutch oven over a high heat. Add the chicken pieces to the pan and cook for 5 minutes until evenly browned. Remove from the pan and set aside.

Reduce the heat to medium, add the sausage slices and cook, stirring, for 4–5 minutes until browned. Remove with a slotted spoon and add to the chicken.

Add a little more oil to the pan if necessary and fry the onion, celery, pepper, and garlic for 5–6 minutes until lightly browned. Add the spice mix and bay leaf and fry for a further 2 minutes. Stir in the rice.

Return the chicken and sausage to the pan, pour in the stock, and add a little salt. Bring to the boil, cover the pan with a tight fitting lid, and simmer gently for 20 minutes. Remove the lid, scatter the shrimp/prawns over the top, cover again, and cook for a further 5 minutes. Remove the pan from the heat and serve scattered with the cilantro/coriander and some lemon wedges.

Coq au vin

Originating from the great wine-growing region of Burgundy, once upon a time coq au vin (cockerel cooked in wine) would have been a peasant dish. In the 1970s it became a bistro icon and today is cooked worldwide. Obviously a Burgundy red is the ideal wine to use, but any full-bodied fruity red wine will work. Serve the casserole with creamy mashed potato. Start this recipe a day ahead.

750-ml bottle red wine

3¼ lb./1.5 kg free-range chicken

7 oz./200 g pearl onions, peeled

2 large carrots, sliced

2 large stalks/sticks of celery, trimmed and sliced

½ teaspoon black peppercorns, lightly bruised

2 bay leaves, bashed

2 sprigs of fresh thyme, bashed

6 tablespoons/90 ml olive oil

9 oz./250 g smoked bacon piece, rind removed and diced

9 oz./250 g small button mushrooms, left whole or halved

1 tablespoon all-purpose/plain flour

4 tablespoons tomato paste/purée

1¼ cups/300 ml chicken stock (see page 19)

2 tablespoons freshly chopped flat-leaf parsley

sea salt and freshly ground black pepper

creamy mashed potato, to serve

SERVES 4

A day ahead, place the wine in a 4-quart/litre Dutch oven and bring to the boil. Boil for 5 minutes until the alcohol is burnt off and the wine slightly reduced. Let this cool completely. Cut the chicken into 8 pieces and place in a bowl. Add the onions, carrots, celery, peppercorns, and herbs and pour over the cold wine. Cover the pan and put in the fridge to marinate overnight.

The next day, carefully pick out the chicken pieces, shake off any excess liquid (back into the pan), and dry the pieces on paper towels. Meanwhile, strain the marinade into a bowl and allow the vegetables to sit in the strainer/sieve to dry. Clean and dry the Dutch oven.

Preheat the oven to 325°F/140°C fan/160°C/Gas 3.

Heat half the oil in the Dutch oven over a high heat, add the diced bacon, and fry for 3–4 minutes until golden. Stir in the mushrooms and season. Fry for a further 3–4 minutes until the mushrooms are golden, then remove from the pan with a slotted spoon and set aside.

Season the chicken pieces well. Heat the remaining oil in the pan until hot. Add the chicken pieces and fry in batches for 5–6 minutes, turning until browned all over. Remove to a plate and discard all but 1 tablespoon of the oil. Reduce the heat to low, add the vegetable mixture to the pan and fry for 5–6 minutes until lightly browned.

Stir the flour into the tomato paste/purée until smooth and then add to the pan, stirring over a medium heat for 1–2 minutes until it is really thick and dry. Gradually pour in the strained marinade wine and stock, stirring constantly, until the mixture boils and thickens and you have a smooth sauce.

Return the chicken to the pan, return to the boil, and cover the pan. Transfer to the preheated oven and cook for 45 minutes. Return the bacon and mushrooms to the pan, cover, and cook for a further 15 minutes until the chicken is really tender. Scatter over the parsley and serve the casserole with some creamy mashed potato.

Whole pot-roast chicken with lemon, olives & sweet spices

A whole roast chicken with Moroccan flavorings is delicious and slightly unusual. The skin on the breast is separated from the flesh underneath in order to make space for the rich buttery stuffing that melts into the bird. This keeps it beautifully moist, whilst adding a wonderful flavor. You can serve it with a side of roasted sweet potato fries or the more traditional couscous, or if you like, serve with both.

3¾ lb./1.75 kg free-range chicken

4 sprigs each of fresh rosemary and fresh oregano, bashed

4 bay leaves, bashed

2 lemons

scant ½ cup/100 g unsalted butter, softened

½ cup/50 g pitted green olives, finely chopped

1 garlic clove, crushed

¾-inch/2-cm piece of root ginger, peeled and finely grated

½ teaspoon ground cinnamon

¼ teaspoon ground turmeric

½ teaspoon freshly ground black pepper

1 tablespoon clear honey

a handful of cilantro/coriander leaves

sea salt

couscous and/or sweet potato fries, to serve

SERVES 4

Preheat the oven to 400°F/180°C fan/200°C/Gas 6.

Place the chicken on a board and carefully slip your fingers under the skin at the neck end of the breast, separating it from the flesh. This will make a pocket for the butter mixture. Cut a couple of slashes into each leg/thigh. Season the cavity of the chicken and pop half the rosemary and oregano, the bay leaves, and half of 1 lemon inside.

Place the butter in a bowl and beat in the olives, garlic, ginger, spices, pepper, and some salt until evenly combined. Push as much of the butter up under the loosened skin as possible, spreading it flat. Spread the remaining butter over the legs and thighs of the chicken and down into the slashes. You can leave the chicken to marinate in the fridge for several hours at this stage, if wished.

Cut the remaining lemons into chunks and place in the base of an oval 5–6-quart/litre Dutch oven, along with the remaining herbs, then place the chicken on top. Cover the pan, transfer to the preheated oven, and cook for 30 minutes, then remove the lid and cook for a further 30 minutes until the chicken is golden and cooked through (pierce the thickest part of the chicken with the tip of a sharp knife and check the juices run clear). Remove the pan from the oven and transfer the chicken to a serving platter. Wrap in foil and rest for 10 minutes.

Using a slotted spoon, remove the herbs and lemons from the cooking juices. Tip the pan gently onto one side, then spoon away and discard as much of the fat as you can, leaving the chicken juices only. Place the pan over a medium heat and stir in the honey until dissolved. Pour the juices over the chicken and scatter with the cilantro/coriander leaves. Serve carved into portions with some couscous and roasted sweet potato fries.

Deep-fried Southern-style chicken with sriracha mayonnaise

I like using a Dutch oven for deep-frying because the weight and rigidity of the pan give me great confidence when heating the oil to a high temperature. Remember it may take a little longer than a regular pan to get to temperature, but once there, you can happily keep it at the correct temperature by reducing the heat to low. Once the chicken pieces are fried to a golden crust, they will need to be cooked for a final few minutes in a hot oven to ensure they are cooked through. Start this recipe a day ahead.

8 small skinless chicken thigh fillets, about 1 lb. 2 oz./500 g in total

1 cup/250 ml buttermilk

1 cup plus 2 tablespoons/150 g all-purpose/plain flour

1½ teaspoons sea salt

1½ teaspoons mustard powder

1 teaspoon dried thyme

1 teaspoon smoked paprika

1 teaspoon celery salt

½ teaspoon freshly ground black pepper

sunflower oil, for frying

dill pickles, to serve

SRIRACHA MAYONNAISE

2 free-range egg yolks

2 teaspoons freshly squeezed lemon juice or white wine vinegar

2 teaspoons Dijon mustard

1 teaspoon sea salt

¾ cup/200 ml pure olive oil (or a mixture of extra virgin olive oil and sunflower oil)

2–3 tablespoons sriracha or other chili/chilli sauce

SERVES 4

A day ahead, place the chicken fillets in a shallow dish. Pour over the buttermilk, cover, and marinate in the fridge overnight—this will help to tenderize the chicken. The next day, remove the chicken from the fridge and return to room temperature for 30 minutes.

Make the mayonnaise. Pop the egg yolks, lemon juice, mustard, and salt into a bowl and whisk until frothy. Very gradually add the oil, whisking constantly until the sauce is thick and glossy. Add the sriracha sauce to your taste. Cover and set aside.

Preheat the oven to 350°F/160°C fan/180°C/Gas 4 and line a baking sheet with foil.

Combine the flour, salt, mustard powder, dried thyme, smoked paprika, celery salt, and black pepper in a bowl. Carefully remove the chicken thighs from the buttermilk and immediately dip into the flour mixture, making sure they are completely coated.

Pour sunflower oil into a 4-quart/litre Dutch oven to a depth of 2 inches/5 cm and heat until it reaches 350°F/180°C on a sugar thermometer (or a cube of bread, dropped into the oil, crisps in 20 seconds). Deep-fry the chicken pieces, in batches, for 2 minutes on each side until crisp and golden. Drain on paper towels and, once all the pieces are fried transfer them to the prepared baking sheet. Place them in the preheated oven to cook through for 5 minutes.

Serve the chicken pieces with the sriracha mayonnaise and some dill pickles.

Quail braised in Marsala with grapes & chestnuts

The sweet, almost spicy flavor of the Marsala paired with chestnuts and fruity grapes makes this quite a sophisticated dish, with the little birds blanketed in bacon and their lovely rich gravy. Parboiling the pearl onions before adding them to the stew serves two purposes: it makes peeling them far easier and ensures that they are tender.

4 quail (each about 5½ oz./150 g)

4 sprigs of fresh tarragon

8 streaky smoked bacon slices/rashers, rind removed

16 small pearl onions, unpeeled

3½ tablespoons/50 g butter

1 tablespoon olive oil

⅓ cup/100 ml Marsala or sweet sherry

1 cup/250 ml chicken stock (see page 19)

3½ oz./100 g cooked chestnuts

3½ oz./100 g seedless red grapes

1 tablespoon freshly chopped tarragon

sea salt and freshly ground black pepper

sautéed potatoes and arugula/rocket salad, to serve (optional)

SERVES 4

Preheat the oven to 375°F/170°C fan/190°C/Gas 5.

Season the quail inside and out with salt and pepper and pop a tarragon sprig into each body cavity. Wrap 2 slices of bacon around each bird and secure in place with toothpicks/cocktail sticks.

Place the onions in a saucepan of cold water, bring to the boil, simmer for 1 minute, then drain and refresh them under cold water. Drain again, pat dry, and remove the skins.

Melt 2 tablespoons/30 g of the butter and the olive oil together in a 3-quart/litre Dutch oven over a medium-high heat. Add the quail, breast side down, and fry for 5 minutes until evenly browned. Remove the quail from the pan and set aside.

Add the onions to the pan and fry for 10 minutes until soft and golden. Return the quail to the pan and add the Marsala, bring to the boil, and cook for 2–3 minutes to burn off the alcohol. Stir in the stock and bring back to the boil. Cover the pan and transfer to the preheated oven. Roast for 15–20 minutes until the quails are cooked through (test with a metal skewer inserted into the thigh meat, once removed the juices should run clear and the metal will be hot to the touch).

Add the chestnuts, grapes, and chopped tarragon to the pan, cover, and cook on the stovetop for a further 5 minutes until the grapes are softened. Remove the pan from the heat and very carefully transfer the quail, grapes, and vegetables to a warm platter. Cover loosely with foil and keep warm.

Place the pan on a high heat and simmer the juices for 5 minutes until reduced by about half. Lower the heat to a gentle simmer and whisk in the remaining butter until the sauce is thickened slightly and glossy.

Remove the toothpicks/cocktail sticks from the quail, then divide the quail, vegetables, and grapes between serving plates and drizzle over the gravy. Serve with the salad and sautéed potatoes.

Duck & sausage cassoulet

Another French classic, this hearty bake includes sausage (traditionally from Toulouse), cooked white beans, and a duck leg confit (or duck preserved in fat). Confit is available from specialist food stores. Cassoulet was the name of the dish used to cook the stew, but a Dutch oven is equally well suited. The rich meaty stew is topped with a blanket of crispy breadcrumbs to soak up the wonderful fatty flavors. Start this recipe a day ahead.

1½ cups/250 g dried haricot or cannellini beans

2 tablespoons olive oil

4 Toulouse sausages, or other quality pork sausages

3½ oz./100 g smoked back bacon slices/rashers, cut into lardons

1 onion, finely chopped

2 garlic cloves, crushed

14-oz/400-g can chopped tomatoes

1½ cups/350 ml chicken stock (see page 19)

2 sprigs of fresh rosemary

4 duck confit (see introduction)

sea salt and freshly ground black pepper

crisp green salad, to serve

TOPPING

3 tablespoons duck fat

2½ cups/150 g coarsely ground fresh white breadcrumbs

2 tablespoons freshly chopped flat-leaf parsley

1 garlic clove, crushed

SERVES 4

A day ahead, place the beans in a bowl and cover with plenty of cold water. Leave to soak overnight.

The next day, drain the soaked beans, rinse well, and place in a large saucepan. Add enough cold water to come at least 4 inches/10 cm above the beans and bring to the boil. Simmer for 45–50 minutes or until just tender. Drain well and set aside.

Preheat the oven to 375°F/170°C fan/190°C/Gas 5.

Heat the oil in a 5-quart/litre Dutch oven over a high heat. Add the sausages and fry for 5 minutes, turning often until browned. Remove from the pan and set aside.

Add the bacon and onion to the pan and fry over a medium heat for 6–8 minutes until golden. Add the garlic and fry for 2–3 minutes. Stir in the tomatoes and stock and bring to a simmer. Add the sausages, rosemary sprigs, cooked beans, duck confit, and season. Bring to the boil, then transfer to the preheated oven and cook, uncovered, for 1–1½ hours or until the beans and duck are very tender. There should be little or no stock left.

Meanwhile, make the topping. Heat the duck fat in a medium skillet/ frying pan, add the breadcrumbs, and stir-fry over a medium heat for 5 minutes until they are all evenly golden. Add the parsley and garlic and cook for a further 1 minute.

Remove the casserole from the oven and scatter over the crumb mixture. Let sit for 10 minutes, then serve accompanied by a crisp green salad.

Slow-braised duck with spices, soy sauce & pears

Duck and fruit are old friends—think of the French bistro classic duck à l'orange. Here the duck is slow-braised in spices, herbs, and aromatics until tender, then left to cool before it is crisped in a hot oven. The pears are braised in the delicious sweet juices and served with jasmine rice. East meets West in duck heaven.

1 onion, roughly chopped

2 leeks, trimmed and thickly sliced

4 garlic cloves, bashed

3/4-inch/2-cm piece of root ginger, sliced and bashed

2 sprigs of fresh thyme, bashed

6 star anise, lightly bashed

2 cinnamon sticks, lightly bashed

3 1/4 lb./1.5 kg whole duck

1 teaspoon Chinese 5 spice powder

1/4 teaspoon Sichuan peppercorns, lightly bashed

1 teaspoon each sea salt and freshly ground black pepper

approx. 1 cup/250 ml chicken stock (see page 19)

3/4 cup/150 g soft brown sugar

1/3 cup/100 ml fish sauce

3 tablespoons dark soy sauce

2 tablespoons rice wine vinegar

3 firm pears, peeled, cored, and quartered

sliced scallions/spring onions and cilantro/coriander leaves, to garnish

jasmine rice, to serve

SERVES 4

Preheat the oven to 450°F/210°C fan/230°C/Gas 8. Line a baking sheet with parchment paper and set aside.

Place the onions, leeks, garlic, ginger, thyme, and whole spices in a 6-quart/litre Dutch oven. Pierce the duck skin all over (especially the breast) with a metal skewer. Combine the Chinese 5 spice powder, Sichuan pepper, and salt and rub all over the duck skin.

Place the duck on top of the vegetables and add 3 1/2 tablespoons/50 ml water. Transfer the pan to the preheated oven and cook for 15 minutes, uncovered, rendering the fat. Then reduce the oven temperature to 300°F/120°C fan/140°C/Gas 2, cover the pan with the lid, and bake for 1 1/2–2 hours or until the meat is very tender. Transfer the duck to a board and set aside to cool for 30 minutes. Increase the oven temperature to 400°F/180°C fan/200°C/Gas 6.

Strain the remaining duck pan juices through a strainer/sieve, pressing down lightly to extract as much juice as you can. Discard the vegetables. Remove as much fat as possible from the drained liquid. Measure the juices and make up to 1 1/4 cups/300 ml with the chicken stock, if necessary. Set aside.

Using poultry shears or a sharp knife, cut the cooled duck in half down the breastbone and backbone. Transfer the halves, skin side up, to the prepared baking sheet, spoon some of the reserved stock over the duck halves (about 3 tablespoons will be enough), and transfer to the oven. Roast for 15 minutes, basting every 5 minutes until the duck skin is crisp and golden and the flesh heated through.

Place the remaining stock and the sugar in a saucepan and bring to a gentle simmer, stirring to dissolve the sugar. Stir in the fish sauce, soy sauce, and vinegar. Place the pears in the pan and simmer, stirring from time to time, for 10–15 minutes until the pears are tender.

Cut the duck halves into portions, place on a serving dish, add the pears and the pan juices. Scatter over some sliced scallions/spring onions and cilantro/coriander leaves and serve with jasmine rice.

Roasted turkey breast with prosciutto & cranberry gravy

Turkey breast meat can be a little dry, especially when it is cooked as part of a whole bird. Here the breast only is stuffed, wrapped in prosciutto, and cooked as a dish in itself. Depending on availability, you can use either 1 large turkey breast of around 3¼ lb./1.5 kg or 2 x 1 lb. 6 oz./750 g smaller breast fillets. Serve with this fruity festive gravy and your favorite vegetable accompaniments.

3¼ lb./1.5 kg turkey breast fillet (or 2 smaller fillets), skinned

2 tablespoons each of freshly chopped rosemary and sage

2 garlic cloves, crushed

grated zest of 2 lemons

4 tablespoons/60 ml extra virgin olive oil

12 large slices prosciutto

1¾ tablespoons/25 g butter

CRANBERRY GRAVY

1 tablespoon all-purpose/plain flour

½ cup/125 ml white wine

1 cup/250 ml chicken stock (see page 19)

4 tablespoons/75 g cranberry sauce

sea salt and freshly ground black pepper

SERVES 8

Preheat the oven to 400°F/180°C fan/200°C/Gas 6.

Take the turkey and, using a sharp knife, slice a pocket into the thicker side as far as you can without cutting it in half. Mix the rosemary, sage, garlic, lemon zest, 2 tablespoons of the oil, and salt and pepper together and spread the mixture into the prepared pocket. Wrap the whole breast in slices of prosciutto and secure in place at ¾-inch/2-cm intervals with kitchen string.

Heat the butter and remaining oil together in an oval 4-quart/litre Dutch oven and sear the turkey roll for 5 minutes until golden all over. Transfer the pan to the preheated oven and roast for 40 minutes or until the juices run clear when spiked with a skewer. Remove the pan from the oven and carefully lift out the turkey roll. Wrap in a double layer of foil and rest for 10 minutes.

Meanwhile, make the gravy. Place the pan on a medium heat on the stovetop, add the flour, and stir for 30 seconds until blended. Gradually whisk in the wine, stirring until the mixture comes to the boil. Simmer for 5 minutes, then stir in the chicken stock and cranberry sauce. Cook for a further 5 minutes until the sauce is thickened slightly and glossy, adjust seasoning to taste.

Pour any turkey juices collected in the foil into the gravy, then carve the breast and serve with cranberry gravy.

Note: If using smaller turkey breast fillets, you only need to cook them for about 25 minutes.

Creamy turkey & mushroom puff pastry pie

What to do with leftover turkey at Thanksgiving or Christmas? This pie is the perfect solution. Normally you would use a pie dish, but the Dutch oven works just as well for this. If you have mini dishes, you can easily make individual pies instead—cut the pastry into small circles the size of the dishes and cook for about 20 minutes.

6 tablespoons/90 ml olive oil

9 oz./250 g button mushrooms, wiped and quartered

1 onion, finely chopped

2 leeks, trimmed and thinly sliced

2 garlic cloves, crushed

2 teaspoons freshly chopped thyme

2 tablespoons/30 g butter, softened

3½ tablespoons/30 g all-purpose/plain flour, plus extra for dusting

2 teaspoons mustard powder

2 cups/500 ml chicken stock (see page 19)

¾ cup/200 ml crème fraîche

14 oz./400 g leftover cooked turkey meat, shredded

3½ oz./100 g cooked ham, shredded or diced

2 tablespoons freshly chopped tarragon

10-oz./275-g packet readymade puff pastry

sea salt and freshly ground black pepper

EGG GLAZE

1 egg yolk

1 tablespoon milk

SERVES 4–6

Heat half the oil in a round 2–3-quart/litre Dutch oven over a high heat. Add the mushrooms and a little salt and pepper and stir-fry for 2–3 minutes until golden but not releasing their juices. Remove with a slotted spoon and set aside. Reduce the heat to medium. Add the remaining oil and fry the onion, leeks, garlic, thyme, and some salt and pepper for 6–8 minutes until really soft but not browned.

Beat the butter, flour, and mustard powder together to form a paste. Stir into the pan and cook for 1 minute. Gradually stir in the stock and then the crème fraîche until you have a smooth mixture. Bring slowly to the boil, stirring constantly, until the sauce is thickened. Remove from the heat and stir in the turkey, ham, mushrooms, tarragon, and salt and pepper to taste. Cover the surface with plastic wrap/clingfilm and allow to cool for 30 minutes, then discard the plastic wrap/clingfilm.

Preheat the oven to 425°F/200°C fan/220°C/Gas 7.

Roll the pastry out on a lightly floured surface to about ½ inch/1 cm larger than the rim of the Dutch oven, trimming the pastry into a round (use the trimmings for decoration). Very carefully lay the pastry in the pan to completely cover the surface of the pie filling. Make a hole in the middle. Press down into the pan around the edges.

For the egg glaze, beat the yolk and milk together until smooth. Brush the pastry top with glaze (add any trimmings and glaze these, too). Bake in the preheated oven for 30–35 minutes until the pastry is puffed up, golden, and the filling bubbling below. Serve immediately.

Chicken baked in coconut milk

This is a variation on a classic Thai curry. A whole chicken is slow-cooked in coconut milk with aromatics and the sweet, sour, and savory flavors of fish sauce, sugar, and lime juice that we love so much. If you like to add a little fire to your curry, simply pop a couple of chiles/chillies into the pan along with the other aromatics.

2 tablespoons sunflower oil

3¼ lb./1.5 kg free-range chicken

1¾ cups/400 ml coconut milk

1¼ cups/300 ml chicken stock (see page 19)

6 makrut lime leaves, bashed

2 stalks of lemongrass, roughly chopped

4 garlic cloves, smashed

¾-inch/2 cm piece of root ginger, sliced

3 tablespoons fish sauce

1 tablespoon light soy sauce

4 tablespoons grated palm sugar or soft brown sugar

freshly squeezed juice of 1 lime

sea salt and freshly ground black pepper

jasmine rice, to serve

SERVES 4

Preheat the oven to 350°F/160°C fan/180°C/Gas 4.

Heat the oil in an oval 4–5-quart/litre oval Dutch oven and fry the chicken, breast side down, for 10 minutes until lightly browned. Remove the pan from the heat, then carefully spoon away and discard all but about 1 tablespoon of the oil.

Add the remaining ingredients to the pan, return to the heat, and bring to the boil. Cover and transfer the pan to the preheated oven and bake for 50 minutes. Remove the lid and bake for a further 10 minutes until the chicken is cooked through (pierce the thickest part of the chicken with the tip of a sharp knife and check the juices run clear) and the pan juices thickened slightly.

Season to taste, then serve the chicken and strained pan juices with some boiled jasmine rice.

POULTRY

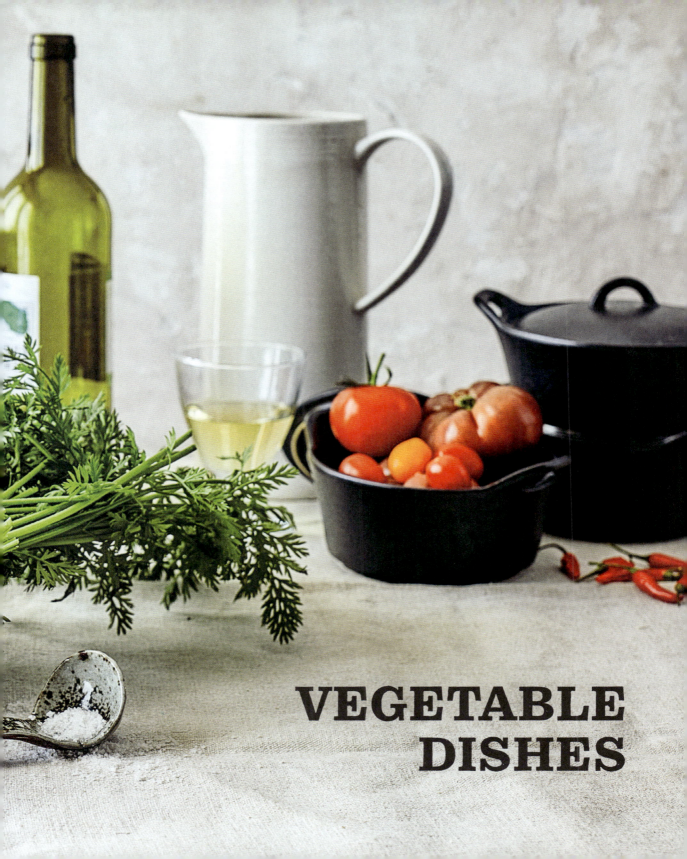

VEGETABLE DISHES

Braised fennel caponata

A Sicilian classic, this vegetable stew is similar to a French ratatouille with the addition of sugar and vinegar for that typical agrodolce flavor (see page 56). The depth of flavor in the vegetables (traditionally deep-fried first) comes from frying them all separately, followed by a very quick braise in a tomato sauce. If available, buy a variety of red pepper called Ramiro, typically grown throughout the Mediterranean region—it is sweeter than round peppers, but either work well.

⅓ cup/100 ml olive oil

2 large heads fennel, trimmed and sliced

1 red Ramiro pepper, seeded and sliced

1 yellow bell pepper, seeded and sliced

1 medium eggplant/aubergine, trimmed and diced into ¾-inch/2-cm cubes

1 onion, finely sliced

1 stalk/stick of celery, finely chopped

¾ cup/200 g strained tomatoes/passata

½ cup/50 g pitted green olives

1 tablespoon capers

2 tablespoons granulated/caster sugar

3½ tablespoons/50 ml white wine vinegar

1 tablespoon toasted pine nuts

sea salt and freshly ground black pepper

fresh oregano, to garnish (optional)

SERVES 4–6

Heat 2 tablespoons of the olive oil in a 2–3-quart/litre Dutch oven over a high heat. Add the fennel and fry, stirring, for 3–4 minutes until softened. Remove with a slotted spoon and set aside. Add a little more oil to the pan and fry the red and yellow peppers for 2–3 minutes until softened, then remove with a slotted spoon. Add a further 2–3 tablespoons of oil and fry the eggplant/aubergine, stirring, for 5 minutes until soft and golden. Remove with a slotted spoon.

Lower the heat to medium and add the remaining oil to the pan. Fry the onion and celery for 5 minutes until softened. Add the tomatoes, olives, capers, and some salt and pepper and simmer gently for 10 minutes until the sauce has thickened a little.

Return all the vegetables to the pan and cook for a further 4–5 minutes. Add the sugar and vinegar, stir well, and remove from the heat. Allow to cool and serve at room temperature garnished with the toasted pine nuts and some fresh oregano, if wished.

Dan dan noodles with tofu & Chinese cabbage

I find stir-fries, supposedly quick and easy dishes, surprisingly difficult—mastering the art of cooking the vegetables so that they are evenly crisp yet tender is no mean feat and one done far better in smaller portions, so this recipe only serves 2. If serving more, cook it in two batches, one after the other, so the results will be perfect.

- 2 tablespoons dark soy sauce
- 1 tablespoon hoisin sauce
- 1 tablespoon black or white rice vinegar
- 1 tablespoon clear honey
- 1 tablespoon tahini paste
- 7 oz./200 g dried Chinese egg noodles
- 4 tablespoons/60 ml sunflower oil
- 5½ oz./150 g firm tofu, diced
- ¾-inch/2-cm piece of ginger, shredded
- 4 scallions/spring onions, trimmed and thinly sliced
- 2 baby bok choy/pak choi, thickly sliced
- 3½ oz./100 g Chinese cabbage, shredded
- a handful of cilantro/coriander leaves
- black sesame seeds, to serve

CHILI OIL

- 4 tablespoons/60 ml sunflower oil
- 1 tablespoon sesame oil
- 3 large garlic cloves, roughly chopped
- 1 teaspoon dried hot red pepper/chilli flakes
- 1 tablespoon Sichuan peppercorns, bashed

SERVES 2

Start by making the chili/chilli oil. Place all the ingredients in a small saucepan and bring to a very gentle simmer (hardly a simmer, more of a shimmer). Cook gently for 5 minutes or until the garlic is just starting to turn golden. Remove from the heat, allow to cool, and then strain into a clean bowl, discarding the garlic. Set aside.

Combine the soy sauce, hoisin, vinegar, honey, tahini, and 1 tablespoon cold water in a bowl. Stir really well to dissolve the tahini. Set aside.

Place the noodles in a bowl and pour over plenty of boiling water. Leave to soak for 5 minutes or until the noodles have rehydrated. Drain, place in a warmed clean bowl, and stir in 2–3 teaspoons of the chili/chilli oil. Cover and keep warm.

Meanwhile, heat the sunflower oil in a round 4-quart/litre Dutch oven over a medium-high heat. Add the tofu and stir-fry for 4–5 minutes until crisp and golden, then remove from the pan with a slotted spoon. Add the ginger and scallions/spring onions and stir-fry for 20 seconds until fragrant. Add the bok choy/pak choi and Chinese cabbage and stir-fry for 30 seconds until starting to wilt. Return the tofu to the pan and then stir in the soy sauce mixture. Cook through for 1 minute until everything is heated through.

Divide the noodles between serving bowls and spoon over the tofu and vegetables, cilantro/coriander leaves and a drizzle more chili/chilli oil. Serve garnished with the sesame seeds.

Bean & pea paella with mint salsa verde

This is the perfect summer paella-style dish with its multitude of beans and peas rounded off with a piquant minty herb salsa. It is a great al fresco sharing dish, and vegans could easily serve it with a tofu-based aïoli.

4 tablespoons/60 ml olive oil

2 garlic cloves, crushed

2 tomatoes, seeded and finely chopped

2 teaspoons sweet paprika

¼ teaspoon saffron strands

1¾ cups/350 g arborio rice

scant 4 cups/900 ml vegetable stock

5½ oz./150 g green beans, trimmed and halved

1 heaping cup/150 g shelled fava/broad beans

1 cup/150 g shelled peas

½ cup/50 g pitted black olives

sea salt and freshly ground black pepper

lemon wedges and aïoli, (see page 34) to serve

MINT SALSA VERDE

1 bunch of fresh mint (about 1 oz./ 30 g)

½ bunch of fresh flat-leaf parsley (about ½ oz./15 g)

1 garlic clove, chopped

1 tablespoon capers, drained and washed

1 teaspoon Dijon mustard

2 teaspoons white wine vinegar

⅔ cup/150 ml extra virgin olive oil

SERVES 4–6

Heat the oil in a 3-quart/litre Dutch oven over a medium heat, add the garlic and fry for 30 seconds or until it starts to soften (be careful not to let it burn). Add the tomatoes, paprika, saffron, and a little salt and pepper and cook for about 5 minutes until the tomatoes and oil start to separate.

Scatter the rice over the tomato mixture, stir well, and cook for 2 minutes. Add the stock, bring to the boil, and cook, uncovered, over a medium-low heat for 10 minutes. Scatter both types of beans and the peas over the top of the rice, cover the pan, and cook for a further 10–15 minutes until the rice is tender, the vegetables cooked, and the stock absorbed.

Meanwhile, make the salsa verde. Place all the ingredients in a food processor or blender with some salt and pepper. Purée to form a smooth paste. Adjust the seasonings to taste.

Remove the pan from the heat, scatter over the olives, then cover with a clean dish/tea towel and leave to sit for 5 minutes. Drizzle over some of the salsa verde and serve with lemon wedges and aïoli, if wished.

Braised squash with mushrooms & crispy choi sum leaves

A lovely braised vegetable and noodle dish with Asian flavors. Choi sum is a Chinese green-leafed vegetable similar to broccoli. The stalks and stems are cooked in the broth, whilst the tender leaves are baked until crisp and golden. As an alternative, you could use regular broccoli florets and kale leaves for baking.

5½ oz./150 g choi sum or broccoli (see introduction)

2 teaspoons sesame oil

2 teaspoons sesame seeds

4 tablespoons/60 ml vegetable oil

9 oz./250 g shiitake mushrooms, trimmed and halved if large

1 large onion, sliced

2 garlic cloves, finely chopped

¾-inch/2-cm piece of root ginger, peeled and grated

⅓ cup/100 ml Shaoxing rice wine

1 lb. 10 oz./750 g butternut squash, peeled, seeded and cut into large chunks (about 1 lb. 2 oz./500 g flesh)

2 cups/500 ml vegetable stock

4 tablespoons/60 ml dark soy sauce

2 tablespoons mirin

7 oz./200 g soba noodles

sea salt

SERVES 4

Preheat the oven to 350°F/160°C fan/180°C/Gas 4 and line a large baking sheet with parchment paper.

Cut the choi sum into stalks and florets and separate the tender leaves. Place the leaves on the baking sheet with the sesame oil and seeds, adding a pinch of salt. Stir well and arrange in a single layer where you can (if using kale, rub the oil into the leaves). Bake in the preheated oven for 5–7 minutes, stirring halfway through, until the leaves are crisp and lightly golden. Remove from the oven and leave to cool.

Heat 3 tablespoons of the vegetable oil in a 3-quart/litre Dutch oven over a high heat. Add the shiitake and fry for 5 minutes until golden. Remove with a slotted spoon and set aside. Reduce the heat to medium.

Add the remaining vegetable oil to the pan and fry the onion, garlic, and ginger for 10 minutes until softened. Add the rice wine and simmer for 2–3 minutes to burn off the alcohol. Place the squash pieces in the pan with the mushrooms and pour in the stock, soy sauce, and mirin. Bring to a gentle simmer, cover, and cook for 10 minutes. Add the choi sum stalks and florets and cook for a further 5 minutes until the vegetables are tender.

Meanwhile, cook the noodles according to packet instructions in a saucepan of lightly salted boiling water. Drain well and divide between soup bowls. Spoon over the stew and top each one with a sprinkling of the crispy choi sum leaves. Serve immediately.

Tartiflette

This dish appears on almost every restaurant menu in the mountainous regions of eastern or central France. A casserole of potatoes, bacon, cream, and cheese, tartiflette is the perfect antidote for a day on the ski slopes. Reblochon cheese, made locally from cow's milk, is perfect as it melts into pools of gooeyness. It is utterly delicious. If you are unable to buy Reblochon there are several options to choose, such as Gruyère, Fontina, Raclette, or a combination of a hard cheese and mozzarella works well too.

1 lb. 2 oz./500 g medium waxy potatoes, such as Charlotte

1 tablespoon olive oil

4 thick slices/rashers of smoked bacon, rind removed, diced

1 red onion, thinly sliced

1 garlic clove, crushed

2/3 cup/150 ml crème fraîche or sour cream

1/2 teaspoon black pepper

1 lb. 2 oz./500 g Reblochon cheese (see introduction for alternatives), thinly sliced

sea salt

hunks of crusty bread and a green salad, to serve

SERVES 4

Preheat the oven to 400°F/180°C fan/200°C/Gas 6.

Peel the potatoes, then place in a 2-quart/litre Dutch oven and cover with plenty of cold water. Bring to the boil and cook for 10–12 minutes or until al dente. Drain and immediately refresh under cold water. Pat dry and cut into 3/4-inch/2-cm chunks. Set aside. Rinse and dry the pan. Set aside.

Heat the oil in a large skillet/frying pan over a medium heat and fry the bacon for 5 minutes until lightly browned. Add the onion, garlic, and a little salt and cook for 5 minutes until softened. Add to the potatoes and stir in the crème fraîche and pepper. Stir well.

Spoon half the mixture into the Dutch oven and top with half the Reblochon. Add the remaining potato mixture and remaining cheese. Transfer to the preheated oven and bake, uncovered, for 25–30 minutes, or until golden and bubbling. Serve with crusty bread to mop up the juices and a green salad on the side.

Note: If you wish to cook the tartiflette in 4 individual 9-oz./250-ml pans, reduce the cooking time to 20 minutes.

Creamy onion & goat cheese risotto with herbs

Unusually for a risotto, here the stock in which the rice is cooked is made from a purée of slow-braised sweet onions, adding an intensity of flavor to the final dish. This sweetness is perfectly balanced by the sharpness of the goat cheese and lovely aromatic flavor of the vibrant green herb oil. You can vary the herbs according to your taste or their availability.

2 lb. 4 oz./1 kg white onions
2 tablespoons olive oil
2 sprigs of fresh rosemary
5 tablespoons/75 g butter
2 large garlic cloves, crushed
1½ cups/300 g arborio rice
2½ oz./75 g soft goat cheese
⅔ cup/50 g freshly grated Parmesan
sea salt and freshly ground black pepper

HERB OIL
2 oz./50 g mixed fresh herbs, to include flat-leaf parsley, basil, and tarragon (or your favorite combo)
⅓ cup/100 ml extra virgin olive oil

SERVES 4

Start by making the herb oil. Bring a medium saucepan of water to the boil, add the herbs and as soon as the water returns to the boil, remove from the heat, strain, and reserve the herbs and water. Immediately refresh the herbs under cold water and then drain again. Squeeze out excess water and dry the herbs on paper towels. Place the herbs, oil, and a little salt and pepper in a blender and blitz until as smooth as possible and a vibrant green. Set aside.

Measure the reserved herb water—you will need 5 cups/1.25 litres so either discard some or add more water as necessary. Return to the same saucepan.

Reserve 1 onion for later; finely slice the remaining onions. Place the sliced onions in a cold 3-quart/litre Dutch oven with the olive oil, rosemary, salt and pepper. Cover and cook over a medium-low heat for 15–20 minutes until the onions are soft and translucent. You will need to stir from time to time, but try not to let too much steam escape.

Once the onions have softened, add the herb water, bring to the boil, and simmer for 5 minutes. Cool, then purée using an immersion/stick blender. Pass the stock through a fine strainer/sieve into a saucepan (not a Dutch oven), pressing down on the pulp. Bring to a gentle simmer.

Make the risotto. Finely chop the reserved onion. Melt the butter in a 2–3-quart/litre Dutch oven over a medium heat and fry the onion, garlic, and a little salt and pepper for 5 minutes until soft. Add the rice and cook for 2–3 minutes, stirring constantly. Gradually start adding the hot onion stock to the risotto, a ladleful at a time, letting the stock be absorbed before adding the next ladleful, continuing to stir for 20 minutes until the rice is al dente.

Add any remaining stock, the goat cheese, and Parmesan and stir well; the risotto should be beautifully creamy. Let sit for a few minutes, then divide between serving bowls and stir in a spoonful or two of the herb oil.

Baked pumpkin & spelt risotto

Unlike risotto rice, spelt grains do not need to be stirred constantly. As the grain cooks, it does become tender but retains a lovely "bite," adding texture to the finished dish. This makes it ideal for baking in the oven. You will need to buy a pumpkin at least 1 lb. 10 oz./750 g in weight to give you 12 oz./350 g flesh.

4 tablespoons/60 ml extra virgin olive oil
1 onion, chopped
2 garlic cloves, crushed
1 tablespoon freshly chopped rosemary, plus extra to garnish
10½ oz./300 g spelt berries
12 oz./350 g pumpkin flesh, grated
4 cups/1 litre vegetable stock
⅔ cup/50 g freshly grated Parmesan, plus extra to serve
¼ cup/50 g mascarpone
sea salt and freshly ground black pepper
a little butter, to serve

SERVES 4

Preheat the oven to 350°F/160°C fan/180°C/Gas 4.

Heat the oil in a 2–3-quart/litre Dutch oven over a medium heat and fry the onion, garlic, rosemary, salt and pepper for 5 minutes until softened. Add the spelt berries and stir-fry for 1 minute until all the grains are glossy.

Add the pumpkin and stir well, then pour in the stock and bring to the boil. Cover the pan and transfer to the preheated oven. Bake for 45 minutes, then carefully remove the lid and check the amount of liquid left. If it is almost gone, cover and bake for a final 15 minutes, or if there is still a fair amount of the liquid, bake uncovered for a further 15 minutes. At this point the grains will be al dente.

Remove the pan from the oven and stir in the Parmesan and mascarpone. Cover and allow to sit for 5 minutes. Season to taste and serve at once dotted with a little butter, a scattering of rosemary sprigs, and some extra Parmesan, if wished.

Tip: Spelt berries are readily available from either your supermarket or from health food stores; alternatively buy online.

Mac 'n' cheese

This version of the classic macaroni cheese can be made in individual mini Dutch ovens if you want (reduce the baking time to 20 minutes). If you are vegetarian, you could either omit the bacon or use your favorite vegan bacon instead. For a crispier topping you can pop it under a hot broiler/grill just before serving.

- 2½ cups/250 g macaroni
- 3¼ cups/750 ml whole/full-fat milk
- 2 bay leaves
- 2 sprigs of fresh thyme, bashed
- a little freshly grated nutmeg
- 3½ tablespoons/50 g butter
- 4½ oz./125 g smoked bacon slices/rashers, rind removed, chopped
- 1 onion, finely chopped
- 6 tablespoons/50 g all-purpose/plain flour
- 1 cup plus 2 tablespoons/100 g freshly grated Cheddar
- 4 tablespoons freshly grated Parmesan
- generous ½ cup/50 g dried breadcrumbs (or panko crumbs)
- sea salt and freshly ground black pepper
- crisp green salad, to serve

SERVES 4

Plunge the pasta into a large saucepan of lightly salted, boiling water and cook according to the packet instructions until al dente. Drain well and set aside.

Place the milk in a saucepan with the bay leaves, thyme sprigs, nutmeg, and a little salt and pepper. Heat the milk gently until it just comes to the boil, then immediately remove from the heat. Let it sit for 15 minutes, then strain and discard the herbs.

Preheat the oven to 375°F/170°C fan/190°C/Gas 5.

Melt the butter in a 3–4-quart/litre Dutch oven, add the bacon, and fry over a medium heat for 3–4 minutes until golden. Remove with a slotted spoon and set aside. Add the onion and fry gently for 5 minutes until softened. Stir in the flour and cook for 1 minute. Gradually add the strained milk, stirring constantly, until the mixture is smooth. Bring to the boil, still stirring, and cook for 2 minutes. Season to taste.

Stir in the cooked macaroni, bacon, Cheddar and half the Parmesan. Combine the remaining Parmesan with the breadcrumbs and scatter over the top of the macaroni. Transfer to the preheated oven and bake uncovered for 15–20 minutes until the cheese is bubbling and golden brown. Serve with a crisp green salad.

Pasta e fagioli

This is an Italian pasta and bean dish (fagioli meaning bean in Italian), cooked in a rich tomato sauce and served topped with grated Parmesan. It is a hearty dish, more a stew than a soup. As well as a good grating of fresh Parmesan, it is lovely drizzled with a fruity extra virgin olive oil. Start this recipe a day ahead.

1¼ cups/200 g dried cranberry/borlotti or cannellini/haricot beans

2 onions

1 bay leaf

4 tablespoons/60 ml extra virgin olive oil

5½ oz./150 g pancetta or smoked bacon, rind removed, diced

1 large carrot, diced

1 large potato, diced

2 stalks/sticks of celery, diced

2 garlic cloves, finely chopped

2 teaspoons freshly chopped thyme

1 teaspoon freshly chopped rosemary

14-oz./400-g can strained tomatoes/passata

2 tablespoons tomato paste/purée

7 oz./200 g small conchiglie or ditali pasta

1–2 tablespoons freshly chopped basil

sea salt and freshly ground black pepper

freshly grated Parmesan and a little extra virgin olive oil, to serve

SERVES 6

A day ahead, place the beans in a large bowl and cover with cold water. Leave to soak overnight.

The next day, drain and rinse the beans and place in a 4-quart/litre Dutch oven. Add plenty of cold water to cover the beans by at least 4 inches/10 cm. Cut 1 onion in half and add to the pan with the bay leaf. Bring the water to a rolling boil, then simmer, uncovered, for 45 minutes or until the beans are al dente. Drain the beans, reserving 5 cups/1.25 litres of the liquid but discarding the onion and bay leaf.

Finely chop the remaining onion. Heat the olive oil in the pan over a medium heat and fry the pancetta for 3–4 minutes until crisp and golden. Remove from the pan with a slotted spoon and set aside.

Add the chopped onion, carrot, potato, celery, garlic, herbs, and salt and pepper to the pan and fry over a medium heat for 10 minutes until softened slightly, stirring occasionally to prevent them sticking. Add the cooked beans, strained tomatoes/passata, tomato paste/purée, and reserved cooking liquid. Bring to the boil, then cover and simmer over a low heat for 30 minutes until the sauce is thick and rich.

Stir the pasta and reserved pancetta into the pan, return to a gentle simmer, and cook for a final 10–12 minutes until the pasta is al dente. Stir in the basil and season to taste. Spoon into individual soup bowls and top each one with Parmesan and olive oil.

Baked savory bread & four-cheese pudding with beet jam

A savory cheesecake mixture, or if you like, a cheesy custard, is poured over slices of day-old baguette and baked until firm and golden. The richness and heartiness of the dish is perfectly offset by the tangy beet/beetroot relish. A side of green salad is the ideal accompaniment. I've made individual puddings, but if you prefer, you can make one large one.

3½ tablespoons/50 g butter, plus extra for greasing

2 leeks, trimmed and thinly sliced

1 garlic clove, crushed

1 teaspoon freshly chopped thyme

1½ cups/350 g cream cheese

1¼ cups/250 g crème fraîche

2 cups/500 ml whole/full-fat milk

4 eggs, beaten

generous ¾ cup/75 g grated Cheddar or Gruyère

scant ½ cup/50 g Gorgonzola or Roquefort, crumbled

a little freshly grated nutmeg

1 medium baguette (about 14 inches/35 cm in length)

2 tablespoons grated Parmesan

sea salt and freshly ground black pepper

green salad, to serve (optional)

BEET JAM

7 oz./200 g raw beets/beetroot, peeled and grated

1 small onion, thinly sliced

⅔ cup/100 ml red wine vinegar

½ cup/100 g dark soft brown sugar

1 teaspoon sea salt

SERVES 4

Start by making the beet/beetroot jam. Place all the ingredients in a saucepan with 4 tablespoons/60 ml water, bring to the boil, and simmer over a medium-low heat for 25–30 minutes or until the liquid has evaporated and the mixture is slightly sticky. Set aside to cool.

Melt the butter in a skillet/frying pan over a medium heat and gently fry the leeks, garlic, thyme, and salt and pepper for 5–6 minutes until softened. Remove from the heat.

Lightly butter 4 x 9-oz./250-ml (or a 2–3-quart/litre) Dutch ovens. In a bowl, beat together the cream cheese, crème fraîche, milk, and eggs until smooth. Stir in the Cheddar, Gorgonzola, nutmeg, cooled leeks, and a little salt and pepper.

Cut the baguette into ½-inch/1-cm thick slices, divide between the prepared pans, and pour the cheese custard over the top, pressing the bread slices down into the pans. Set aside for 30 minutes to soak.

Preheat the oven to 400°F/180°C fan/200°C/Gas 6.

Scatter each pudding with a little of the grated Parmesan and transfer the pans to the preheated oven. Bake for 30–35 minutes (or for 50–60 minutes for a large pudding) or until the puddings are puffed up and golden. Cover the pans after about 25 minutes if the tops are becoming too brown. Test with a skewer inserted into a pudding—it is cooked when the skewer comes out clean.

Remove from the oven and allow to sit for 5 minutes. Serve with the beet/beetroot jam and a crisp green salad.

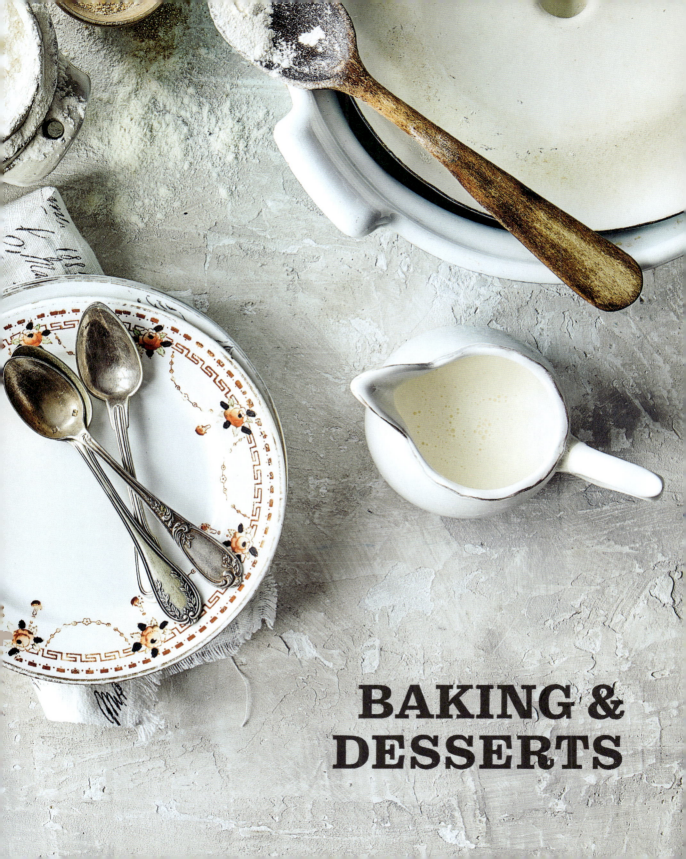

BAKING & DESSERTS

No-knead bread

Here is my version of the classic no-knead bread from Sullivan Street Bakery in New York. The inclusion of ground toasted barley grains adds a fabulous nutty flavor and aroma to this simple loaf—it really is almost too good to be true. Start this recipe a day ahead.

- 2 tablespoons/25 g barley grains (available from health food stores)
- 3 cups/400 g unbleached white bread flour, plus extra for dusting
- 1 teaspoon salt
- ½ teaspoon instant dried yeast
- 1¼ cups/300 g warm water

MAKES 1 LOAF

A day ahead, toast the barley grains in a skillet/frying pan, stirring for 2–3 minutes until golden and smelling nutty. Allow them to cool and then grind to a fine powder. Set 1 tablespoon aside for this recipe and store the rest in a sealed jar (it lasts until it is used up).

Sift the flour and the tablespoon of roasted barley powder into a bowl and stir in the salt. Dissolve the yeast in the warm water and then add to the flour. Work the mixture with your hands until it is sticky (it will be really wet and sticky). Cover the bowl with plastic wrap/clingfilm and leave for 12–18 hours in a draft-free spot in your kitchen.

The next day, tip the dough out onto a well-floured surface (you will likely need to help it out) and work it gently into a round. The dough will still be very soft, but this is exactly what you want as this is what gives the bread its open and slightly waxy texture.

Transfer the dough to a well-floured proofing basket or a bowl lined with a well-floured clean dish/tea towel. Cover with plastic wrap/clingfilm and leave to rise for 3 hours until the dough is doubled in size and you can see little pockets of air on top.

Preheat the oven to 450°F/210°C fan/230°C/Gas 8. Place a round 2-quart/litre Dutch oven (about 8¾ inches/22 cm across) into the oven to heat up for 20 minutes.

Once the dough is ready, place a sheet of parchment paper over the dough bowl and a board on top of the paper. Carefully and gently invert the bowl so that the bread tips lightly out onto the paper.

Very carefully remove the hot pan from the oven and the lid from the pan. Lower the dough, still on the baking paper, down into the hot pan, being very careful not to touch the sides. Very gently score the top with a sharp knife to form a pattern. Immediately cover with the lid, return to the oven, and bake for 30 minutes. Remove the lid and bake for a further 5 minutes until the bread is browned. Transfer the bread to a wire rack and leave until cold. Serve in slices, plain or toasted, with butter.

Tip: For metric cooks, here that I have weighed the water in grams—this is far more accurate when making bread.

Walnut, fig & honey bread

This easy bread has a lovely cake-like texture made by grinding most of the walnuts before adding them to the flour, whilst the figs bring a perfect sweet note and together they impart a really lovely flavor to the bread. Delicious slathered with lightly salted butter.

1¼ cups/125 g walnut halves

¾ cup/175 ml warm water

1½ teaspoons dried yeast

2 tablespoons clear honey

2 tablespoons walnut oil

1 teaspoon salt

1¾ cups/250 g white unbleached white bread flour, plus extra for dusting

heaping ⅓ cup/50 g wholemeal bread flour

⅔ cup/100 g dried figs, chopped

a little olive oil, for greasing

MAKES 1 LOAF

Preheat the oven to 400°F/180°C fan/200°C/Gas 6.

Place the walnuts on a baking sheet and cook in the preheated oven for 5–6 minutes until toasted. Set aside to cool. Roughly chop the walnuts and set ½ cup/50 g to one side.

Meanwhile, place the water, yeast, honey, walnut oil, and salt in a small bowl and stir to dissolve the yeast. Stir in 2 tablespoons of the white flour until blended. Set aside for 10 minutes until the mixture begins to bubble.

Place the remaining white flour and wholemeal flour in a food processor with the main quantity of chopped walnuts and process until you have a fine crumb-like mixture. Transfer to a large bowl, make a well in the middle, and stir in the frothed yeast mixture. Bring the mixture together in the bowl until you have a soft dough. Cover the bowl with plastic wrap/clingfilm and set aside for 30 minutes.

Transfer the dough to a lightly floured surface and knead for 5 minutes, then start adding the figs and remaining chopped walnuts in batches, continuing to knead for a further 2–3 minutes after each addition until they are all incorporated and the dough is smooth and elastic. Place the dough in a lightly oiled bowl, cover with plastic wrap/clingfilm, and leave to rise for 1–1½ hours or until doubled in size.

Preheat the oven to 425°F/200°C fan/220°C/Gas 7. Place a round 2-quart/litre Dutch oven (about 8¾ inches/22 cm across) with its lid in the oven to heat up for 20 minutes.

Once the dough is risen, place a sheet of parchment paper over the dough bowl and a board on top of the paper. Carefully and gently invert the bowl so that the bread tips lightly out onto the paper.

Carefully remove the hot pan from the oven and the lid from the pan. Lower the dough, still on the paper, into the hot pan, being very careful not to touch the sides. Very gently score the top with a sharp knife to form a pattern. Immediately cover with the lid, return to the oven, and bake for 30 minutes. Remove the lid and bake for a further 10 minutes until the bread is browned. Transfer the bread to a wire rack and leave to go cold. Serve in slices with lots of butter.

Zucchini, scallion & feta cornbread

Cornbread is, as the name suggests, made using cornmeal, combined with baking powder and baking soda/bicarbonate of soda rather than yeast to help it rise. This produces a highly flavored savory bread with a lovely crumbly texture. It can be plain, or as it is here, laced with vegetables, herbs, and cheese to make it truly delicious. You can grease the sides of your Dutch oven, but also line the base with greased parchment paper to avoid the bread sticking.

7 oz./200 g zucchini/courgettes, trimmed

¾ cup/100 g all-purpose/plain flour

1 tablespoon baking powder

½ teaspoon baking soda/bicarbonate of soda

1⅔ cups/250 g medium cornmeal/polenta

1 teaspoon sea salt

3 eggs, beaten

scant 1¾ cups/400 ml buttermilk

5½ oz./150 g feta, crumbled

⅓ cup/25 g freshly grated Parmesan

2 scallions/spring onions, trimmed and finely chopped

2 tablespoons freshly chopped cilantro/coriander

freshly ground black pepper

mixed tomato and arugula/rocket salad, to serve (optional)

MAKES 1 LOAF

Preheat the oven to 400°F/180°C fan/200°C/Gas 6. Grease a 2-quart/litre Dutch oven (or a 9½-inch/24-cm oven) and then line the base with greased parchment paper.

Finely grate the zucchini/courgettes and squeeze out any liquid using a clean dish/tea towel.

Sift the flour, baking powder, and baking soda/bicarbonate of soda into a bowl and stir in the cornmeal/polenta and salt. Beat the eggs and buttermilk together and stir into the dry ingredients using a wooden spoon to make a smooth batter. Finally, stir in the zucchini/courgettes, feta, Parmesan, scallions/spring onions, cilantro/coriander, and a little pepper until evenly combined.

Spoon the mixture into the prepared pan. Bake, uncovered, in the preheated oven for 30 minutes until the cornbread is risen and golden and a skewer, inserted in the middle, comes out clean and dry. Cool in the pan for 5 minutes, then turn out to cool on a wire rack.

Serve warm in slices with a mixed tomato and arugula/rocket salad.

Mini Dutch pancakes with raspberries & passion fruit syrup

This baked pancake is thought to have been invented in around 1900 by a Seattle cafe owner. It is similar to a popover or Yorkshire pudding batter, but lighter in texture and sweetened with sugar. Traditionally it is baked in mini Dutch ovens (as the name implies) but you can also cook it as a whole pancake in a larger pan (see tip). You can vary the toppings as desired and these can be anything from fresh fruit to a chocolate or caramel sauce (see page 138).

3 eggs, beaten

½ cup/125 ml whole/full-fat milk

1 teaspoon vanilla extract

3¼ tablespoons/45 g unsalted butter, melted

½ cup plus 1 tablespoon/80 g all-purpose/plain flour

1 tablespoon confectioner's/icing sugar, plus extra for dusting

a pinch of salt

2 tablespoons/30 g salted butter, diced

⅓ cup/100 ml heavy/double cream

1 scant cup/100 g fresh raspberries

PASSION FRUIT SYRUP

⅓ cup/100 ml passion fruit pulp (from about 3 large passion fruit)

3½ tablespoons/50 ml freshly squeezed orange juice

5 tablespoons/60 g granulated/caster sugar

SERVES 4

Start by making the passion fruit syrup. Place the passion fruit pulp, orange juice, and sugar in a small saucepan and heat gently, stirring, to dissolve the sugar. Simmer for 5–6 minutes or until it is syrup-like. Set aside to cool.

Preheat the oven to 400°F/180°C fan/200°C/Gas 6.

Make the pancakes. Place the eggs, milk, vanilla extract, and the melted unsalted butter in a food processor and blend until combined. Sift in the flour, confectioner's/icing sugar, and salt and blend again until you have a totally smooth batter.

Divide the salted butter between 4 x 8½-oz./250-ml individual Dutch ovens and place on a baking sheet. Transfer to the preheated oven and heat the butter for 2–3 minutes until melted and hot. Very carefully pour the batter into the pans and cook for 10–12 minutes until the pancakes are puffed up and golden.

Meanwhile, beat the heavy/double cream in a small bowl until firm. Once the pancakes are cooked, transfer the dishes to charger plates (being careful as they will, of course, be very hot). Divide the cream between the pancakes and drizzle with the passion fruit syrup. Scatter over the raspberries and serve dusted with confectioner's/icing sugar.

Tip: If you wish, this can be cooked as one large pancake in a 2-quart/litre pan (or a 8¾-inch/22-cm diameter oven) for about 18 minutes until puffed up and golden.

Baked orchard fruit cobbler with cinnamon crème fraîche

This is such a versatile dish as it can easily be adapted to any time of year, using pretty much any fruit you like. For example, in summer when berries and stone fruit are at their best, combine peaches and raspberries, or earlier in the summer cherries and apricots.

8 large plums

3 pears

2 cups/250 g fresh blackberries

1 tablespoon crème de cassis (optional)

4 tablespoons soft brown sugar

COBBLER TOPPING

1⅓ cups/180 g all-purpose/plain flour

1½ teaspoons baking powder

a pinch of salt

⅓ cup/75 g unsalted butter, diced

¼ cup/50 g granulated/caster sugar

½–⅔ cup/125–150 ml buttermilk

CINNAMON CRÈME FRAÎCHE

¾ cup/150 g crème fraîche

2 teaspoons confectioner's/icing sugar, sifted

a little ground cinnamon

SERVES 6

Preheat the oven to 375°F/170°C fan/190°C/Gas 5.

Halve, stone, and thickly slice the plums. Peel, core, and thinly slice the pears. Wash and dry the blackberries. Place the fruit in a bowl, add the cassis (if using) and brown sugar, and stir well to combine. Transfer the fruit to a 2-quart/litre Dutch oven.

To make the topping, sift the flour, baking powder, and salt into a bowl and rub in the butter to make fine crumbs. Stir in the sugar. Work in enough buttermilk to bring the mixture together to make a slightly sticky dough. Spoon mounds of the topping over the fruit layer, allowing some fruit to remain uncovered.

Transfer the pan to the preheated oven and bake uncovered for 30–35 minutes until the topping is risen and golden and the fruit is oozing rich juices. Check halfway through and cover the pan with the lid if the top is beginning to over-brown.

Meanwhile, make the cinnamon crème fraîche. Stir the crème fraîche, sugar, and cinnamon together until combined. Serve with the fruit cobbler.

Pumpkin, fig & maple syrup steamed pudding

A Dutch oven is the ideal pan in which to steam a sponge pudding. The water in the base of the pan will happily simmer away whilst the pudding, in its own basin, cooks to perfection. Here grated pumpkin adds both a lovely rich flavor and a moist texture to the sponge.

softened butter, for greasing

¾ cup/125 g dried figs, chopped

½ cup/75 g dried dates, stoned and chopped

scant ½ cup/50 g golden raisins/sultanas

1 cup/250 ml boiling black tea, freshly made

1 teaspoon baking powder

½ teaspoon baking soda/bicarbonate of soda

⅓ cup/75 g butter, softened

6 tablespoons/75 g soft brown sugar

2 eggs, lightly beaten

1½ cups/200 g self-rising/raising flour

1 teaspoon ground mixed spice

7 oz./200 g peeled pumpkin, finely grated (about 1 lb. 4 oz./550 g before peeling)

4 tablespoons/75 g maple syrup or golden syrup, plus extra to serve

vanilla custard, cream, or ice cream, to serve

SERVES 6

Grease a 6-cup/1.5-litre pudding basin generously with the softened butter. Cut a circle of parchment paper about 2 inches/5 cm larger than the pudding basin and cut 2 sheets of foil, again about 2 inches/5 cm larger than the basin. Make a pleat along the middle of the paper, then do the same with the double layer of foil.

Place the dried fruits in a bowl and add the boiling tea, baking powder, and baking soda/bicarbonate of soda. Stir well and set aside for 15 minutes to froth.

Beat the butter and sugar together until pale and creamy, then gradually beat in the eggs a little at a time until smooth. Fold in the flour and mixed spice until combined (it will be quite dry at this stage), then stir the pumpkin and dried fruit mixture and the soaking liquid into the bowl until evenly blended.

Spoon the maple syrup into the base of the prepared pudding basin and carefully spoon in the sponge mixture, covering the syrup layer. Top with the pleated parchment paper, then the double layer of pleated foil and tie this tightly in place with kitchen string, making sure you have a piece long enough to go twice around the basin and leave enough to make a handle.

Place a small trivet (or a baking ring) in the base of an 8-quart/litre Dutch oven and place the pudding basin on top of the trivet. Carefully pour in enough boiling water to come two-thirds of the way up the side of the basin. Place on a high heat and bring the water back to the boil. Reduce the heat to very low, cover the pan, and steam for 2½–3 hours. Check after 2½ hours—press a skewer into the pudding, through the foil and the paper right down to the base. Leave it there briefly, then pull it out. It should be clean and very hot to the touch (don't burn yourself) to be sure it is cooked.

Once cooked, carefully remove the basin from the pan and set aside for 10 minutes. Remove the string, foil, and paper and invert the pudding onto a serving plate. Drizzle over some extra syrup. Serve in wedges with homemade vanilla custard, cream, or ice cream.

New Orleans cinnamon donuts with chocolate sauce

These cute rectangular donuts are a specialty of New Orleans and popular during Mardi Gras. They are light and fluffy and I love them drizzled with this cinnamon-flavored chocolate sauce.

2 teaspoons dried yeast

2/3 cup/150 ml warmed milk

2½ tablespoons/30 g granulated/caster sugar

2½ cups/350 g unbleached white bread flour, plus extra for dusting

1 teaspoon vanilla extract

3½ tablespoons/50 g unsalted butter, melted

2 eggs, beaten

CHOCOLATE CINNAMON SAUCE

2/3 cup/150 ml heavy/double cream

1 cinnamon stick, bashed

3½ oz./100 g bittersweet/chocolate 70% cocoa solids

1 tablespoon/15 g unsalted butter

1 tablespoon dark corn syrup/golden syrup

CINNAMON SUGAR

1 tablespoon confectioner's/icing sugar

½ teaspoon ground cinnamon

MAKES APPROXIMATELY 40

Place the yeast and warm milk in a bowl with a pinch of the sugar and 1 tablespoon of the flour. Stir well to dissolve the yeast and set aside in a warm spot until bubbles appear on the surface, about 10 minutes.

Sift the remaining flour into a large bowl and make a well in the middle. Add the frothed yeast mixture, vanilla extract, melted butter, and eggs and work the mixture together with your hands to form a quite sticky dough. Cover the bowl with plastic wrap/clingfilm and rest for 15 minutes.

Transfer the dough to a well-floured surface and knead for 5 minutes until smooth. Shape the dough into a ball, place in a lightly oiled bowl, cover with plastic wrap/clingfilm, and leave to rise for 1 hour or until doubled in size.

Preheat the oven to 350°F/160°C fan/180°C/Gas 4.

To make the sauce, place the cream and cinnamon in a small pan and heat gently until it just reaches the boil. Set aside to infuse for 15 minutes. Discard the cinnamon. Return the cream to the heat, add the chocolate, butter, and corn syrup/golden syrup and heat very gently, stirring, until the chocolate is melted and the sauce is smooth. Keep warm.

Very gently remove the risen dough from the bowl and use your fingers to press to form a rectangle about ¾ inch/2 cm thick. Using a sharp knife, cut the dough into 1¼-inches/3-cm squares. You should have about 40 in all.

Pour oil to a depth of at least 2 inches/5 cm (but not more than 3¼ inches/8 cm) into a 4-quart/litre Dutch oven and heat to 350°F/180°C on a candy/sugar thermometer (or a piece of bread crisps in 20 seconds). Carefully add the dough in batches of 4–5 and fry for 1½–2 minutes, turning halfway through, until puffed up and golden. Drain immediately on paper towels and keep warm in the oven while cooking the rest.

Mix together the confectioner's/icing sugar and ground cinnamon on a plate, add the donuts in batches, and roll lightly in the sugar. Serve drizzled with the chocolate sauce.

Tip: When deep-frying in a Dutch oven, once the oil has reached its required temperature, turn the heat down as low as you can or it will soon become too hot. You can then adjust it up slightly, as necessary.

Upside-down pineapple & coconut cake with rum cream

A Dutch oven provides a great alternative to a regular cake pan for this classic upside-down cake. Once your Dutch oven is hot, the cast iron maintains an even temperature throughout the bake so the oven temperature is set slightly lower than if using a regular cake pan. It is not necessary to line the pan with parchment paper, but oil the sides of the pan to help prevent the sponge layer from sticking.

½ ripe pineapple (about 1 lb. 4 oz./ 600 g)

a little toasted coconut, to decorate

SAUCE

½ cup plus 1 tablespoon/ 125 g butter

scant ⅔ cup/125 g soft brown sugar

a pinch of salt

1 tablespoon pineapple juice

SPONGE

⅔ cup/150 g unsalted butter, softened, plus extra for greasing

1 cup/200 g granulated/caster sugar

a pinch of salt

3 large eggs, lightly beaten

1½ cups/200 g self-rising/raising flour, sifted

1 cup/75 g shredded/desiccated coconut

½ teaspoon baking powder

½ cup/125 ml sour cream or crème fraîche

RUM CREAM

½ cup/100 g mascarpone

3½ tablespoons/50 ml heavy/ double cream

2 tablespoons confectioner's/ icing sugar

1 tablespoon golden rum

SERVES 8–10

Preheat the oven to 325°F/140°C fan/160°C/Gas 3. Rub the softened butter over the insides of a round 2-quart/litre Dutch oven (or 9½-inch/24-cm width).

Peel the pineapple and cut it into ½-inch/1-cm thick slices—you will need 5 slices to cover the base of the pan. Using a small cookie cutter, stamp out and discard the central core. Use the remaining pineapple half to squeeze out the juice—you only need 1 tablespoon.

To make the sauce, put the butter, soft brown sugar, salt, and the 1 tablespoon pineapple juice into a small saucepan and place over a medium heat. Cook, stirring, until the butter is melted and sugar dissolved. Bring to a simmer and cook for 2 minutes until it starts to thicken. Carefully pour the mixture into the greased pan and set aside to cool for 20 minutes, then arrange the pineapple slices in the cooled sauce.

Place all the sponge ingredients in a food processor and blend until smooth. Carefully spoon the mixture over the sauce and pineapple slices, spreading it smooth. Cover the pan with its lid, transfer to the preheated oven, and bake for 40–45 minutes until the cake is risen and firm to the touch. Insert a metal skewer into the center of the cake and remove. The skewer should be clean, if so the cake is cooked; if it is sticky, return to the oven and cook for a further 5–10 minutes.

Remove the pan from the oven, remove the lid, and let it sit for 10 minutes. Place a large plate upside down over the top of the Dutch oven and using oven mitts (or a thick dish/tea towel) very carefully invert the pan to unmold the cake. Allow to cool.

To make the rum cream, place all the ingredients in a bowl and, using an electric mixer, beat together until thickened. Cut the cake into wedges and serve with the rum cream and some toasted coconut.

Index

A
agrodolce sauce 56
aïoli 34
aubergines see eggplant

B
bacon: bacon pangrattato 15
  pea & ham soup 28
  tartiflette 112
beans: bean & pea paella 108
  Boston baked beans 79
  duck & sausage cassoulet 93
  white bean & rosemary soup 15
beef: beef short rib daube 68
  Hungarian goulash 71
  oven-baked meatballs 67
  Vietnamese-style miso, red wine & caramel beef cheeks 64
beet jam 123
bell peppers: Hungarian goulash 71
blackberries: baked fruit cobbler 134
borlotti beans see cranberry beans
Boston baked beans 79
bread: baked savory bread & four-cheese pudding 123
  no-knead bread 126
  walnut, fig & honey bread 129
  zucchini, scallion & feta cornbread 130
broad beans see fava beans
butternut squash: braised squash with mushrooms 111

C
cabbage: cabbage & apple slaw 76
  dan dan noodles with tofu & Chinese cabbage 107
  kimchi 24
Cajun chicken & seafood jambalaya 82
cake, upside-down pineapple & coconut 141
cassoulet, duck & sausage 93
cheese: baked savory bread & four-cheese pudding 123
  creamy onion & goat cheese risotto 115
  mac 'n' cheese 119
  tartiflette 112
chicken: Cajun chicken & seafood jambalaya 82
  chicken baked in coconut milk 101
  chicken dumpling soup 19
  coq au vin 85
  deep-fried Southern-style chicken 89
  Mexican chicken & lime soup 23
  Vietnamese chicken, rice & vinegar soup 31
  whole pot-roast chicken 86
chiles/chillies: chili oil 107
  salsa rossa 42
  Singapore chile crab stir-fry 50
Chinese-style braised fish with clams 37
choi sum, braised squash with 111
cinnamon crème fraîche 134
clams, Chinese-style braised fish with 37
cleaning Dutch ovens 9
cobbler, baked orchard fruit 134
coconut: upside-down pineapple & coconut cake 141
cod, home-salted 46
coq au vin 85
cornbread: zucchini, scallion & feta 130
cotriade 45
courgettes see zucchini
crab: Singapore chile crab stir-fry 50
cranberry/borlotti beans: pasta e fagioli 120
cranberry gravy 97
crème fraîche, cinnamon 134
curry, Sri Lankan fish 41

D
dan dan noodles with tofu & Chinese cabbage 107
donuts, New Orleans cinnamon 138
duck: duck & sausage cassoulet 93
  slow-braised duck 94
dumplings 19, 71

E
eggplant/aubergine: braised fennel caponata 104

F
fava/broad beans: bean & pea paella 108
fennel caponata 104
figs (dried): pumpkin, fig & maple syrup steamed pudding 137
  walnut, fig & honey bread 129
fish: Chinese-style braised fish 37
  cotriade 45
  Sri Lankan fish curry 41
  Tuscan seafood stew 49
  see also monkfish, salmon etc

G
gammon: Boston baked beans 79
garlic: aïoli 34
goulash, Hungarian 71
gravy, cranberry 97
Greek-style lamb 59
green beans: bean & pea paella 108
gumbo, shrimp 27

H
haricot beans see navy beans
herb oil 115
Hungarian goulash 71

J K
jambalaya, Cajun chicken & seafood 82
kedgeree, hot salmon 38
kimchi 24
Korean noodle broth 24

L
lamb: Greek-style lamb 59
  Moroccan lamb 63
  Sicilian agrodolce-stuffed lamb 56
  whole leg of lamb pilaff 60

M
mac 'n' cheese 119
mayonnaise: aïoli 34
  sriracha mayonnaise 89
meatballs, oven-baked 67
Mexican chicken & lime soup 23
mint salsa verde 108
monkfish, oven-braised 42
Moroccan lamb 63
mushrooms: braised squash with 111
  creamy turkey & mushroom puff pastry pie 98
mussels: cotriade 45
  Tuscan seafood stew 49

N

navy/haricot beans:
  Boston baked beans 79
  duck & sausage cassoulet 93
New Orleans cinnamon donuts 138
noodles: dan dan noodles with tofu & Chinese cabbage 107
  spicy Korean noodle broth 24

O

oil: chili 107
  herb 115
okra: shrimp gumbo 27
onions: baked French onion soup 12
  creamy onion & goat cheese risotto 115
  red onion pickle 75

P

paella: bean & pea paella 108
  shrimp paella 34
pancakes, mini Dutch 133
parsley: persillade 68
passion fruit syrup 133
pasta: Greek-style lamb 59
  mac 'n' cheese 119
  pasta e fagioli 120
pea & ham soup 28
pears: baked orchard fruit cobbler 134
  slow-braised duck with 94
peas: bean & pea paella 108
peppers see bell peppers
persillade 68
pickles 64, 75
pies: creamy turkey & mushroom puff pastry pie 98
  smoked fish pies 53

pilaff, whole leg of lamb 60
pineapple: upside-down pineapple & coconut cake 141
plums: baked orchard fruit cobbler 134
pomegranate relish 60
pork: rolled pork belly in cider 72
  slow-cooked pork carnitas tacos 75
  slow roasted pork ribs 76
  spicy Korean noodle broth 24
potatoes: cotriade 45
  home-salted cod with 46
  smoked fish pies 53
  tartiflette 112
prawns see shrimp
pumpkin: baked pumpkin & spelt risotto 116
  pumpkin, fig & maple syrup steamed pudding 137
  roasted pumpkin soup 20

Q

quail braised in Marsala 90

R

ras el hanout 63
raspberries, mini Dutch pancakes with 133
rice: bean & pea paella 108
  Cajun chicken & seafood jambalaya 82
  creamy onion & goat cheese risotto 115
  hot salmon kedgeree 38
  shrimp paella 34
  whole leg of lamb pilaff 60

risotto: baked pumpkin & spelt risotto 116
  creamy onion & goat cheese risotto 115
rum cream 141

S

salmon: hot salmon kedgeree 38
  smoked fish pies 53
salsa rossa 42
salsa verde, mint 108
salt: home-salted cod 46
sausages: duck & sausage cassoulet 93
shrimp/prawns: Cajun chicken & seafood jambalaya 82
  shrimp gumbo 27
  shrimp paella 34
  Tuscan seafood stew 49
Sicilian agrodolce-stuffed lamb 56
Singapore chile crab stir-fry 50
slaw, cabbage & apple 76
smoked haddock:
  smoked fish, bacon & charred corn chowder 16
  smoked fish pies 53
soups 12–31
spelt: baked pumpkin & spelt risotto 116
spinach: smoked fish pies 53
squash, braised 111
Sri Lankan fish curry 41
sriracha mayonnaise 89
steamed pudding: pumpkin, fig & maple syrup 137
stews: beef short rib daube 68
  braised fennel caponata 104
  coq au vin 85
  cotriade 45
  duck & sausage

cassoulet 93
  Hungarian goulash 71
  Moroccan lamb 63
  Tuscan seafood stew 49
  Vietnamese-style miso, red wine & caramel beef cheeks 64
stock, chicken 19

T

tacos, slow-cooked pork carnitas 75
tartiflette 112
tofu, dan dan noodles with 107
tomatoes: agrodolce sauce 56
  Boston baked beans 79
  oven-baked meatballs 67
  pasta e fagioli 120
  Tuscan seafood stew 49
turkey: creamy turkey & mushroom puff pastry pie 98
  roasted turkey breast 97
Tuscan seafood stew 49

U

upside-down pineapple & coconut cake 141

V

Vietnamese chicken, rice & vinegar soup 31
Vietnamese-style miso, red wine & caramel beef cheeks 64

W

walnut, fig & honey bread 129
white bean & rosemary soup 15

Z

zucchini, scallion & feta cornbread 130

Acknowledgments

I feel so lucky to have been given the opportunity to write this book. After what can only be described as a very grim 15 months during the Covid pandemic, lives around the world have changed dramatically. Living in rural France has meant my family and I have largely been unaffected, so I feel very fortunate.

I would like to thank everyone one involved in making this book happen at Ryland, Peters & Small and their continued belief in me as a writer. Thank you to my husband Ian, who is the greatest photographer I know! And thanks must also go to all those who have truly made a difference during 2020 and beyond.